W9-BQS-703

Without Consent

How to Overcome
Childhood Sexual Abuse

Carol Jarvis-Kirkendall
Jeffery Kirkendall

SWAN PRESS, INC.
SCOTTSDALE, ARIZONA

Copyright © 1989 by Swan Press Incorporated

All rights reserved. No part of this book amy be reproduced or utilized in any form or by any means, electronic or mechanical, including photocopying, recording or by any information storage and retrieval system, without permission in writing from the Publisher. Inquiries should be addressed to Permissions Department, Swan Press Inc., P.O. Box 9928 Scottsdale, AZ. 85252.

Library of Congress Cataloging-in-Publication Data
Jarvis-Kirkendall, Carol, 1939-
    Without consent.
      1. Adult child sexual abuse victims.
I. Kirkendall, Jeffery, 1952-   II. Title.
RC569.5A28J37   1989   616.85'83   89-60708
ISBN 0-9615530-0-6

Printed in the United States of America
First Edition

This book is dedicated to our clients

and

to the child within each one of them.

CONTENTS

PREFACE

This book is the result of the authors' fifteen years combined experience working with persons who at some time in their lives have been sexually abused. In a supervisory role and/or in a therapist's role, we have been involved in providing psychological services to approximately fifteen hundred families dealing with the trauma of sexual abuse. This population included both male and female children from as young as two years of age through adults of both genders and as old as eighty years of age. Many of the families contained multiple victims. A conservative estimate of the number of identified victims would be well in excess of two thousand. Note that we say "identified" victims. We have chosen this word because sexual abuse is a trauma which usually affects the entire family system, making victims of all its members.

This book is first and foremost about victims, by victims and for victims. If you are a female victim of childhood sexual abuse, the majority of the text is directed to you. Our messages to recovering victims are as follows:

YOU ARE NOT ALONE

YOU ARE NOT SHAMEFUL

YOU ARE NOT DEFECTIVE

YOU ARE NOT CRAZY

THERE IS HOPE

Our goal can be paraphrased in the words of William Faulkner – that the victim of childhood sexual abuse not only endure, but that she prevail.

This book is also for the family members and the friends of victims—the husbands, parents, children and significant others who have felt the pain and stress of life experiences shared with a victim. It can bring you new understanding of victims you have come across in the past. It can help you to be of aid to victims that you know in the present. It can teach you to identify and understand victims that you will encounter in the future.

Thirdly, this book is for professionals in the mental health field and those in the "helping" professions—social workers, psychologists, clergy, teachers, criminal justice personnel, and others who encounter victims on a professional basis.

The authors apologize for what, on cursory observation, may appear to be a chauvinistic approach to the problem of sexual abuse. It was an editorial decision to identify victims as feminine and victimizers as masculine. This approach to the problem in no way implies that sexual abuse of both male and female children by female victimizers does not occur. In our clinical practice approximately five percent of our adult female clientele have been identified as both victims and victimizers. An astonishing ninety-three percent of our male victimizers were themselves victimized—sexually and/or physically—in childhood. All were abused emotionally and/or spiritually as children by adult males and/or females. If you are an adult male who was victimized in childhood, this book can aid you in your recovery. Many of the dynamics, problems and solutions for female victims apply to male victims as well. There are, of course, differences, but the trauma symptoms and treatment modalities are similar. The authors wish to emphasize that sexual abuse of males in childhood and the victimization of children by adult females are not issues of lesser impact or importance than the subject of this book. They are areas of concern that demand their own forums, and more research.

The nature and extent of the abuse suffered by the victims we have worked with was varied. Some women were victims of isolated incidents of fondling, exposure, or oral contact. Most were victims of repeated offenses ranging in physical trauma from gentle touching to sadistic rape. Some women remembered only one abusive experience; some victims were abused throughout their entire childhood. Most persons' experiences were somewhere in between these two extremes. Many women experienced verbal sexual abuse, psychological sexual abuse, spiritual abuse and/or emotional incest. Many of the victims were physically abused as well as sexually abused. Some were involved in pornography or prostitution. Some were tortured.

The women who are quoted throughout the book were chosen from the many women that we have worked with as clients. They represent a wide spectrum of educational, socioeconomic, ethnic, and religious backgrounds. Minor details have been altered and pseudonyms have been used, but the experiences that they share with you are true. Although dealing with varying degrees of stressful and debilitating issues, only a few of these women have been institutionalized for mental health reasons. All are functioning in the "everyday" world.

The victims were abused, predominantly, by males; some were abused by members of both sexes. The victimizers were persons known to the victims. Almost all were relatives, friends, trusted mentors, or authority figures. Some of the women were victimized by more than one person. Like their victims, the victimizers came from all walks of life and every socioeconomic stratum. Only a small percentage of the victimizers were sadistic psychopaths.

This book is also based on the authors' own perilous and triumphant journeys through their own personal traumas. Half of this partnership was also a victim of childhood sexual abuse. What both of us have learned in our personal relationship and personal growth, together and as individuals, is reflected in our writing. We want to share what we have learned, both personally and professionally, so that all may benefit, therapists as well as victims and their families.

If you were a victim of sexual abuse as a child, there will be times when you will be anxious or angry about what you read in this book. There will be times when you will want to avoid reading it. It is probable that you initially will not recognize some behaviors as your own, or you will deny having engaged in others. These are normal responses. You may experience, while reading, any number of fears—fear of remembering something long-since stuffed away, fear of finding out that there is something wrong with you, fear of not being able to cope with the memories or feelings that may come up in the present or in the future. These are all fears that you can overcome. When you find portions of the text disconcerting, you can put the book aside for a while. You can continue reading when you feel strong again. We assure you that your responses are predictable and normal.

You may ask, "Why should I continue to read this book if I experience difficulties?" Read this book for what it has to offer you as a guide through the healing process of recovery. Mark up the margins. Underline and highlight those portions of the text which are significant to you. Make note of sections which strike a chord for known or unknown reasons. *Be patient* with yourself. Read at whatever pace is comfortable for you. *Be persistent.* There will be many times in the future when rereading portions of the text will provide fresh insights and guidance. We encourage you to seek support and validation in your recovery process through a variety of resources: friends, family, clergy, and mental health professionals. Seek out persons with whom you feel safe in sharing. Confide in those persons whom you believe to be trustworthy. If your first choice of a confidant does not work out, do not be deterred. Take a risk and find another. Child abuse is an abuse of power and control. Now is the time for *you* to exercise *control* of *your* life. Now is the time for *you* to be *empowered.* The timetable for dealing with and triumphing over any obstacles is up to you. You can ask for guidance and support, but no one can do it for you. No one can choose your path for recovery and act upon that path but *you.*

All of the material contained in this book is open to critical examination. We encourage this. The problem of sexual abuse demands public awareness and challenge. More empirical study of the problem of childhood sexual abuse is needed to separate fact from fiction. As a society, we need more information and practical solutions on how a healing process may be effected.

Serious discussion of sexual abuse demands answers to the following questions:

(1) Is sexual abuse a problem of major proportions in this country?

(2) Is a person who was sexually abused as a child by an adult always influenced by that experience?

(3) Is it possible for a person to be a victim of abuse and not remember the abuse or not identify it as abusive?

(4) Can a single sexual abuse experience as a child cause problems for an individual as an adult?

(5) Can a person be sexually abused without being touched?

(6) Can a person appear to be successful outwardly—involved in a primary, monogamous relationship; have close friends, children and family; be sexually active; successfully pursue a career—and also be suffering with problems caused by an abusive childhood?

(7) Can sexual abuse as a child affect a person's adult sexuality and sexual lifestyle?

(8) Can sexual abuse as a child affect areas of a person's adult life other than sexuality?

(9) Are there ways to tell the difference between healthy and unhealthy sexual contact between a child and an adult?

(10) Is there such a thing as a "victim mentality"?

(11) Can an individual's sense of personal spirituality or her concept of God be affected by childhood sexual abuse?

(12) Can a person triumph over the problems caused by an abusive childhood?

Within this book we will present information and testimony that support our contention that the answer to each of the above questions is an emphatic, YES!

ACKNOWLEDGEMENTS

When we began this book in the spring of 1984, we thought that we would complete a manuscript within a year, two years at the very most. At first, when a projected date of completion would arrive and pass, we would experience impatience and frustration. Gradually, however, we began to realize that *Without Consent* had a life and timetable of its own. We discovered that this project was teaching us as much as we hoped to teach others.

Each time we thought that we were close to completion, life presented us with a new lesson. A teenage daughter needed our time, support and love. We had physical disabilities to face and conquer. Critical issues within both our marriage and professional relationships demanded that we face them and work them through. Issues left over from our respective pasts required resolution before we could address new projects. Last but not least, financial challenges threatened to destroy everything for which we had worked so long and hard.

Our faith and courage were constantly challenged and enriched. In retrospect, we can see that each obstacle brought with it a necessary lesson. Each lesson provided wisdom and courage. *Without Consent* is a better book today than it would have been if it had been completed on our timetable. At the time of this first printing it represents a great personal triumph to both of us.

We are wiser and more mature persons for having met and known the extraordinary people who accompanied us on our creative journey.

Tony and Lisa Ebarb became much more than our accountants. They become our mentors and taught us many lessons about humility, faith, money, power, joy and love.

Dr. Gerald Shaw, a colleague and a friend, demonstrated his confidence in us from the beginning. His sense of humor and playfulness effect healing and growth in our lives and the lives of others.

Mary O'Riley, while traveling her own spiritual path, seized a moment within that journey to help make someone else's dream come true.

Deborah and Roy Weymouth recognized that their vision paralleled our own. They suggested that we maximize our talents and effectiveness by joining forces on the journey.

The Reverend Steven Kalas was an untiring source of genius and love. He listened, challenged, advised and encouraged us.

Mary Ford travelled with us throughout our journey, often at great risk to herself. She maintained a courage and enthusiasm for our vision even when we felt weary and discouraged. She never gave up on us.

Andy and DeAnn Staven shared their lives and their resources with us. They were a constant source of encouragement, unwavering in their belief in and support of our ministry.

Kenny Higgins believed in us and supported us at a time of great struggle and change in his own life. He stretched himself and took risks because he had faith in a cause that was bigger than all of us.

Don Wilcox was with us from the very beginning. A man of gentle strength and faith, he often picked us up and carried us when we stumbled. He is in our hearts and prayers every day.

Gary Walton was unfaltering in his confidence and love for us. He went on to experience greater joy in life than he had ever believed possible.

Gerald Burgess, a talented and artistic friend, took a chance on some fellow eccentrics.

Elaine and Vernie Kirkendall, Walter and Sarah Snyder, each had the courage and love to believe in us, even when they did not understand us.

Chris Lawlor provided his cabin as a much needed retreat. It was here that we accomplished much of the actual writing and learned many profound mystical lessons.

Most important of all, we thank our daughter, Marybeth Fowler. She invested in us more than anyone else. She indulged our moods, endured our absences, forgave our impatience and fear, and shared our sacrifices. She courageously confronted the challenges in her own life and regularly inspired us to do the same. During the time that we were writing this book, she matured from a little girl into a confident and competent young woman. It was a joy to behold.

1

YOU ARE NOT ALONE

The first thing I learned (in the Women's Therapy Group) was that I wasn't alone. RHONDA

INTRODUCTION

When we were working in an agency which dealt exclusively with sexual abuse, we had little difficulty in identifying a client's source of problems. Only the most blatant cases of abuse found their way to the agency. Most cases had already been reported to the child protective agencies and police. They were rape, incest, and child molestation situations, and there was seldom any doubt as to whether or not the person had been traumatized. Our therapeutic modality consisted predominantly of short-term interventions to deal with the most obvious traumatic symptoms of abuse.

In our private practice, "hidden" forms of sexual abuse began to come to light. Clients often sought our services for problems other than childhood sexual abuse — anxieties, sleep disorders, depression, and marital problems to name a few. During the therapeutic process it became increasingly common for clients to remember abusive childhood incidents that had been suppressed or repressed. Often clients did not initially identify long-forgotten incidents as abusive. Many had endured subtle forms of sexual abuse which had become powerful, but not obvious, influences in their adult lives. In order to understand the more subtle forms of abuse, we will begin by examining the more obvious ones.

LEGAL DEFINITIONS

In the United States, the criminal justice system's definitions of *Sexual Abuse, Molestation of a Child* and *Incest* vary with each state's criminal code. Most contain generalities and specificities such as the following, which are excerpted from the Arizona Revised Statutes: Title 13, Criminal Code; September, 1982.

SEXUAL ABUSE:
A person commits sexual abuse by intentionally or knowingly engaging in sexual contact with any person not his or her spouse without consent of that person or with any person who is under fifteen years of age and who is not his or her spouse.

MOLESTATION OF A CHILD:
A person . . . knowingly molests a child under the age of fifteen years by fondling, playing with, or touching the private parts of such child or. . . causes a child under the age of fifteen years to fondle, play with, or touch the private parts of such person.

A primary focus in the above definitions is "intentionally or knowingly engaging in sexual contact . . ." A parent or baby sitter who changes diapers or examines a child's genital area for health reasons is not, under normal circumstances, at risk of criminal prosecution. Under these circumstances, it is obviously not the adult's intent to sexually abuse the child. The criminal justice system is designed to prosecute those individuals who use children sexually and do so knowingly.

THE ISSUE OF CONSENT

The criminal justice system is concerned with the issue of "consent" —having a person's permission to be sexual with her. The definition of sexual abuse states that to have sexual contact with someone "not his or her spouse and without consent of that person" is a violation of the law. In many states, this portion of the above definition is similar to what would be defined as a "rape" or "sexual assault" statute. In several states sexual contact with one's spouse without consent is being or has been tested as a violation of the law and re-defined as rape or sexual assault.

The sexual abuse definition also clearly states that persons under fifteen years of age are sexually off limits regardless of so-called "consent." The "15-years-old" distinction is practical in a legal sense since it provides a definitive guideline for the courts in determining culpability. The age distinction is superfluous from a psychological perspective since the fear, pain, and shame experienced by a sexual abuse victim can be equally as devastating before or after her fifteenth birthday.

INCEST:
Persons who are related by blood or marriage who knowingly intermarry, commit adultery or engage in sexual intercourse with each other. (Arizona Revised Statutes.)

The various legal definitions of incest, like those of sexual abuse and molestation, do not address the psychological dimensions of such an experience. Most sexual abuse cases require blatant evidence of intentional abuse. While this is an understandable legal necessity, it can be a psychological tragedy. In most cases a medical doctor must provide evidence such as tissue damage or contusions via a thorough physical examination of the victim.

Those cases which depend upon victim testimony for prosecution are often tenuous. Attorneys and "experts" can cast doubt on the ability of a child to accurately and credibly testify. A general rule is that the younger a child is, the more irrefutable physical evidence is required and the less credible is a child's testimony due to her immaturity. The potential for tragedy is obvious — by the time physical evidence is present, emotional and psychological damage to a child can be extensive and, in extreme cases, lethal.

STATISTIC:
The chief cause of death of sexually abused infants and children in New York City each year is rectal hemorrhage. (Ruth S. and C. Henry Kempe, 1985.)

Some states are seeking to minimize further victimization of a child witness by employing a variety of interventions. Included are videotaping a child's testimony for all parties to view, and/or by allowing a child witness to be in a separate room during the trial proceedings and to give her testimony via closed circuit video.

THERAPEUTIC DEFINITIONS

From a therapeutic perspective, to be sexually abused does not require violent physical contact. To be adversely affected by an experience, a person need only be aggressed against or taken advantage of psychologically. We begin an explanation of this phenomenon by offering definitions of sexual abuse and incest which focus on the psychological dynamics of sexual abuse.

SEXUAL ABUSE:
The involvement of dependent and developmentally immature children and adolescents in sexual activities that they do not fully comprehend, to which they are unable to give informed consent, or that violate social taboos of family roles. (Schechter & Roberge, 1976)

SEXUAL ABUSE:
Contacts or interactions between a child and an adult when the child is being used for the sexual gratification of that adult or another person. Sexual abuse may also be committed by a person under age 18. (The National Center on Child Abuse and Neglect [NCCAN] 1982)

INCEST:
The sexual abuse of a minor by either an adult related to the child by blood or by marriage, or by an adult living within the family unit and perceived by the child as a member of the family. (Carol Jarvis-Fowler, 1979)

Of critical importance in these definitions are (1) the lack of in-formed consent, (2) the developmental immaturity of children, and (3) the breakdown of healthy and nurturing family roles.

ABUSE OF POWER

No child is developmentally equipped to comprehend and emo-tionally handle the ramifications of a sexual encounter with an adult. A child operates in such a situation from a position of almost complete vulnerability to the power of an adult.

> *POWER:*
> Possession of control, authority, or influence over others . . .
> ability to act or produce an effect . . . mental or moral efficacy.
> Power may imply latent or exerted physical, mental, or spiritual
> ability to act or be acted upon. . . Power implies possession of
> ability to wield coercive force, permissive authority, or substantial
> authority. (*Webster's New Collegiate Dictionary*, 1975)

In a sexual encounter between an adult and a child, there exists an inherent imbalance of power. An adult is more powerful and intimidating than most children due to physical size alone. He possesses more verbal resources. He is capable of comparatively sophisticated psychological manipulations. A child is psychologically, developmentally and emotionally less mature than an adult. A child's understanding of the dangers in life and the need for personal boundaries and self-protection is by definition immature. Children are socialized to defer to adult authority—"Respect your elders," "Do what Daddy says," "Grown-ups know better," etc. An adult can induce fear or even terror with a phrase, a gesture or a tone of voice. The implications are clear. An adult possesses the ability to influence, to control, and to victimize a child.

Even in the most "non-threatening" of scenarios, adults assume power by their very presence. A child does not have an understanding of sexuality, knowledge about life experiences, or the emotional maturity to accurately assess the implications of a sexual encounter with an adult.

She does not have the psychological resources required to make a personal evaluation as to the motives or intent of the adult in control of the situation.

NATALIE:

My uncle would masturbate me when I was five years old, and it felt good, and I wanted to feel that pleasurable feeling. I didn't know what it was, but I knew that it made me feel warm and loved.

Natalie was like any child, eager to please and anxious to experience affection. She did not understand her body's responses. It did not occur to her that she was being exploited. She did not know that her victimizer had motives other than being a "good uncle." She interpreted the situation as any child might—What her uncle was doing felt good, and he treated her gently and gave her attention when she cooperated with him.

TINA:

I remember thinking, when I was six years old, "Why did he choose me? What did I do to make this happen?"

JOYCE:

He'd hug me and if I didn't hug him back in just the right way, he'd get mean and hurtful. So I learned real fast how to keep him happy.

Both Tina and Joyce reacted to situations over which they had no control. Their roles were to meet the distorted needs of adults. Tina, using a child's logic, sought to comprehend the reason(s) for her experience. She identified herself as having caused the painful situation that she was experiencing. In Joyce's case, the penalty for non-cooperation was overt. Both Tina and Joyce were taught to do whatever was necessary to keep their victimizers "happy." They were also taught that they would suffer painful consequences if they failed in their roles.

THE VICTIMIZER

Victimizers who are sincerely motivated in a recovery program "discover" or disclose that they have used children as objects for narcissistic purposes. As they mature in the recovery process, they discover the extent to which their purposes have detrimental and destructive consequences for the children.

What prompts a victimizer's behavior? Sexual excitement, an attempt to experience intimacy or self-esteem, anger, control, and the acting out of a sexually addictive pattern are some of the answers. The critical prerequisite in a victimizer's choice of a child as a sexual partner is the fact that a child is in a position of less power. This imbalance of power — the fact that the child is not in control — is the key element of a victimizer's attraction to a child as a sexual partner. A child's trust, vulnerability, and her inability to seriously challenge or confront her victimizer are prerequisites to accomplishing the victimizer's goals.

Every victimizer rationalizes his behavior to some degree — "I was teaching her about sexuality," or "She wanted it as much as I did," or " I was drunk (or stoned, or high) and didn't know what I was doing," or, "She came into my bed and I thought she was my wife," or "My wife wasn't meeting my needs," or, "She was very mature for a five-year-old."

Whatever the rationalization, all of these adults are responsible for having manipulated a child into an experience that she does not fully comprehend, an experience about which she cannot possibly make an informed decision, and an experience in which she is inherently in a position of less power.

CHILDHOOD

The needs of a young person in her formative stage of life (those years labeled "childhood") are to be loved, to belong, and to experience a sense of worth in the eyes of her primary caretakers. In our private practice we have heard countless stories of the extremes to which a child will go in attempting to gain her parents' approval and love. Children who have endured repeated brutalization, isolation and degradation recount repeated attempts to experience love, to be affirmed. It is this passion for life and love that places a child at an insurmountable disadvantage when engaging in any interaction with an adult—especially interactions characterized by a gross misuse of power and control. Regardless of how unthreateningly an adult approaches a child, an adult who engages in sexual behavior with a child is, by definition of the circumstances, a victimizer.

SEDUCTION

SEDUCE:
1. To entice into wrongful behavior; corrupt. 2. To induce to have sexual intercourse. (*The American Heritage Dictionary,* 1976)

The authors take a firm and unequivocal stand regarding the issue of so-called "seductive" behavior by children: Children do not seduce adults.

Children exhibit behaviors that they have been taught in order to receive attention and/or affection. "Seductive" is an adult term that describes adult behaviors. An adult labeling a child as seductive erroneously attributes to a child motives and capabilities that come only with adulthood. Such an adult also implies that accountability for any sexual interactions belongs to the child rather than placing the responsibility where it properly belongs—with the adult. To label a child as seductive implies that a child has equal or greater power in an interaction with an adult.

To reiterate, there are no seductive children—no irresistible temptresses of one or two or ten years of age. There are only adult victimizers, people who are emotionally crippled and/or immature, people who deny responsibility for their behavior, people who claim helplessness under a child's "power," people who project their sexual impulses onto children, and people who consciously or unconsciously relinquish self-control and responsibility.

CHILDREN DO NOT SEDUCE ADULTS.

IMMATURE ADULTS SEDUCE CHILDREN.

BEING NORMAL

One of the most obvious effects of sexual abuse is the persistent concern of a victim that she is not "normal," a fear that she may not even know what "normal" is.

MARIE:

I went looking for "normal." It was like going through life blind-folded. I spent years looking for a "love" experience, but I wouldn't have seen it if I had found it. . . . I kept my secret and "acted" normal. I watched other people and did what they did.

LORI:

I was afraid I'd lose control and become a wild and dangerous person. It became important to appear absolutely "normal." I had no problems.

Obviously, the term "normal" is relative and not necessarily even a recommended goal for any person, abused or not. What is normal to any one person or any particular culture may be quite eccentric to another. It is important to understand that each victim reveals in her quest for "normalcy" that she has been, in her opinion, "changed" in a negative sense, by the abuse, i.e., that she is "damaged," "deviant," or "shameful." Her subjective experience leads her to the conclusion that she is somehow an irreversibly different "person" as a result of her abuse experience(s).

BONNIE:

What kept me in so much turmoil was that I knew what my life was supposed to be about (normal) —Where I came from, what I was supposed to do, where I was going. And everyone thought he (my father) was so wonderful, and I knew otherwise. It confused everything; it didn't make sense. I just couldn't understand!

TINA:

I don't have any idea of what "normal" is. My grandfather abused me when I was very young. I never had any kind of real communication or relationship with my dad. To this day, I've never had a "normal" sexual relationship with a man, or even a pleasurable one. It's kind of sad.

It is sad. Most victims do experience themselves as being "different," alienated from the mainstream of life, or even irreversibly "damaged."

TINA:

I felt like I was the only person in the world that was like I was, and maybe I was there for people to do this to.

It is true that the memory of an abusive experience remains with a person for life. It is not true that such an experience has to be permanently handicapping. Sexual abuse can be, but is not necessarily, a terminal illness. It does not have to mean partial or total disability for those who survive it.

LOUISE:

I don't ever want to forget it (the abuse) again, because I now know that I had a whole lot of strength and courage to go through some of the things that I experienced.

FRAN:

We were strong, to survive those experiences.

HOLLY:

In order to cope now I rely on some of the strengths that got me through then.

STATISTICS

What are the dimensions of the sexual abuse of children in the United States? Available statistics on the prevalence and effects of sexual abuse in this country vary widely, but most tend to support the opinion of a growing population of professionals that it is a "societal secret" of astounding proportions and ramifications. Some of the figures compiled to date are as follows:

* There are thirty-two million adult women in this country who were victims of sexual abuse when they were children. (*Life Magazine,* Summer, 1984)

* One in five girls and one in eleven boys responding to a college questionnaire reported having had a sexual experience of some kind with a much older person during childhood. (Finkelhor, 1979)

* Thirty to forty percent of all children are sexually abused in some way before the age of eighteen. ("He Told Me Not To Tell," King County Rape Relief, 1979)

* One out of four girls are sexually assaulted at least once in growing up. (Lucy Berliner, Harborview Hospital, Seattle, 1979)

* One in four females are sexually assaulted before thirteen. Boys account for ten percent of all reported child assault victims. About ten percent of all sexually assaulted children are younger than five years old. (American Humane Society, 1981)

* One out of five rape victims is under the age of twelve. (American Humane Society, 1981)

* Boys and girls are at equal risk of being sexually assaulted. (Lloyd Martin, Los Angeles Police Department, 1981; A. Nicholas Groth, 1983)

* At least thirty percent of the time the child molester is a relative (experts believe the percentage is higher, but because incestuous incidents are the least likely to be reported, it is difficult to demonstrate this statistically). (American Humane Society, 1981)

* Of one hundred and sixty women treated for sexual dysfunction it was found that ninety percent had been raped during childhood, twenty-three percent by fathers or stepfathers. (Baisden, M. "The World of Rosaphrenia: The sexual psychology of the female, Sacramento, Ca.; Quoted in H. Giarretto's, "The humanistic treatment of father-daughter incest." *Journal of Humanistic Psychology,* Fall, 1978)

* In one of the few studies to compare two groups of women in psychotherapy, one with incest histories and one without, eighty-seven percent of the incest group complained of sexual problems compared to twenty percent of the control group. Seventy-five percent of the victims of father-daughter incest and eighty-five percent of the victims of brother-sister incest specifically reported orgasmic dysfunction (Meiselman, K. *Incest: A psychological study of causes and effects with treatment recommendations.* San Francisco: Jossy Bass, 1979)

* A Minnesota study of adolescent female prostitutes revealed that seventy-five percent had been victims of incest. (Green, R. "Victim of child abuse tells her story," *Boston Globe,* September 9, 1977)

* Seventy percent of young prostitutes were sexually abused as children. (American Humane Society, 1979)

* Seventy-five percent of all prostitutes were victims of incest. (*Plexus Report,* 1980)

* Two million children run away from home each year, and up to half of them do so because they have been abused, primarily sexually. (Ruth S. & C. Henry Kempe, 1985)

* As many as eighty percent of all incidents go unreported, experts estimate. (*The Sun,* San Bernardino, Ca. January 20, 1983)

* Robert L. Geiser, author of *Hidden Victims: The Sexual Abuse of Children*, is more pessimistic, saying that for every case reported, twenty-five go unreported.

In the summer of 1985, a nationwide survey was conducted by the *Los Angeles Times* on the topic of child molestation. Two thousand, six hundred and twenty-seven adults talked about their childhood experiences. The resulting data shatters many of the myths still held by the public about child sexual abuse. Information collected from the 100-question survey indicates that:

* Twenty-seven percent of the women interviewed and sixteen percent of the men said they had been molested as children.

* Fewer than half the victims told someone about the molestation within a year. Only three percent reported the incident to the police or another public agency.

* One in three of the victims said they had never told anyone about the molestation until the survey, most often because they were afraid or ashamed.

"There is a strong suggestion here and elsewhere in the responses that victims do not realize that their own experience is typical, that they believe what happened to them is not what happens to others," said I. A. Lewis, director of the *Los Angeles Times* poll.

SOCIETAL AWARENESS

The crime of childhood sexual abuse touches nearly every family in America. Those who were not victims themselves know someone who was. If we believe even the most conservative estimates as to the rate of occurrence, then there is a case of sexual abuse on every block of every community in this country.

Societal response to sexual victimization is at the point today that treatment of the alcoholic was thirty years ago. It was common at that time for society to treat alcoholism in one of two modalities; (1) for the family and associates of the alcoholic to deny that there was a problem, for them to offer explanations and make excuses for the alcoholic's behavior, and for them to consistently compromise in order to accommodate the alcoholic's behavior and resultant problems; or (2) to disown the alcoholic as a hopeless "drunk."

Drunkenness carried a shameful social stigma. It was a problem that was relegated to persons who were viewed as inherently inferior—the lower socioeconomic classes, the uneducated, and the morally depraved. We know today that it is a severe medical problem of epidemic proportions. As a social problem it cuts across all socioeconomic strata, all educational strata, and all ethnic groups. For alcoholism to be appropriately confronted on a societal level, it had to be brought out of the closet, its realities acknowledged, and its myths challenged.

We can do no less with the problem of childhood sexual abuse. As with the family of an alcoholic, we must admit that we have a problem which affects all our members. Childhood sexual abuse is a social problem of epidemic proportions. Its existence and its incidence is a reflection of our country's internal functioning or dysfunctioning. Critics can distort the true issues by labeling children as seductive. They can minimize the rate of incidence by referring to it as child abuse hysteria. They can discount valuable social criticism by labeling it militant feminist rhetoric. However skeptical the critics remain, a simple truth cannot be denied: A dramatically increasing number of adult women are stepping forward to say, "I was sexually abused as a child and I was hurt by the experience."

2

YOU ARE NOT SHAMEFUL

The knowing is so important. Knowing that we didn't do it, that it was done to us. Knowing that we're not the ones to blame. LANA

INTRODUCTION

In this chapter, we will focus on the characteristics common to sexual abuse victims. We have drawn from our professional training and experiences and from our clients' reports to describe behavior patterns.

"Behavior" is the response of an individual to his/her environment. Behavior encompasses thoughts and emotions as well as actions. A "pattern" is a reliable sample of traits, actions or other features that characterize an individual. It is a predictable repetition of behaviors and/or mental processes.

Not everyone who was sexually abused as a child will have participated in all of the behavior patterns described in this book. All victims, however, will have experienced one or more of the patterns at some time in their lives.

THREE CLASSIC CASES

The following case histories are typical descriptions of childhood sexual abuse. The stories are composites of many persons whom we have seen in therapy. The life circumstances described are not unusual.

There is much we could have added about each character's life.
However, the facts we have presented in each story are those which are
important for learning purposes. We have deliberately not included details
of how each child was sexually abused. It is more important that the
reader be able to identify the issues that these seemingly diverse characters
have in common.

If you were a victim, do not try to fit your own life history into any
one of the stories. You will find similarities to your life experiences in any
or all of these three examples. Any of the family dynamics or abuse
scenarios described can occur within the context of any socioeconomic
group, any ethnic group, and any educational or professional group. Take
notice that all three women were victims of other persons' power and
control. The nature of their respective life circumstances provided few real
choices, certainly no easy ones. As innocent children, they did the best that
they could in situations where someone else had most of the control.

THE STORY OF ANN

Ann was born in a large city on the east coast, the illegitimate
child of a relationship between her mother and a family friend. Ann's
mother, who was very young and dependent when Ann was born, felt
throughout her life that she had brought great shame on her family of
origin, who were Catholic, hard-working and respectable lower middle
class. During Ann's early childhood her mother was involved in numerous
brief relationships with men. These liaisons consisted of Ann and her
mother being abused and then abandoned. The man that Ann's mother
married when Ann was two years old was abusive and alcoholic, but he was
also the only person who had offered her the respectability of marriage.
Ann's mother felt that she was fortunate to have won his favor and was
very fearful of losing the only security and approval she had ever experienced in her life.

Ann's stepfather was physically, emotionally and sexually abusive to
both Ann and her mother almost from the first day. A total dictator in his
family, he was the only person who made rules — or broke them. Ann's

mother was always pregnant or busy with a new baby. Ann was expected
to take care of herself and her five younger siblings.

At the mercy of her stepfather's anger at home, she found escape
and refuge for a while in school. She sometimes hinted to counselors and
friends of her stepfather's sexually abusive behavior. She wanted to tell
someone, but her consistent experience of her stepfather was one of brutality. She greatly feared his retaliation if she revealed his abuse of her. He
had beaten her mother and her on many occasions. He made it quite clear
to Ann that if he did not have her for the sex he wanted, he would pick on
one of her sisters. She was taught that it was her responsibility to protect
the younger children.

Unable to excel in school academically, she began to get attention
with acting out—at first as the class clown, then as the girl who would do
"anything" on a dare. She was soon involved in petty criminal behavior,
sexual promiscuity and experimentation with drugs. When social service
agencies and school officials challenged the dysfunctions in the home, the
family "closed ranks" around Dad and focused on Ann as the problem.

Ann dropped out of school in the tenth grade. She found employ-
ment as a topless dancer and became involved in a series of abusive
relationships with men. Sometimes she accepted money and gifts for her
sexual favors.

At age twenty-five Ann married a man much older than herself.
For a brief time she determined to be sexually faithful to her husband, but
her resolve lasted only a few months before she began seeing other men.
During this time she gave birth to a daughter—not her husband's child.
Ann left her husband after a year and moved in with an Air Force sergeant
who insisted that she supplement their income by prostituting herself. Her
new "boyfriend" also physically abused her and took all of her money. They
parted after a particularly abusive confrontation in which Ann suffered
several fractured ribs. Ann's young daughter was taken away from her by
child protective services and placed with her parents.

Ann is now thirty-one years old and involved in a sexual relationship with another woman. She describes herself as bisexual and states that
she has no problems with sexual functioning (including orgasm.) Her usage
of alcohol and prescription drugs is excessive and causes her to lose time at
her job as a clerk at a convenience market.

Ann denies that she has a problem with either relationships or substance abuse. She states that she can quit her addictions anytime that she chooses to. She visits her daughter sporadically and worries that her stepfather might be abusing her child as he did Ann, but she does not consider herself capable of challenging her parents' authority by removing her daughter from their custody.

THE STORY OF LINDA

Linda was born in a small midwestern town, the youngest child in a family that included three older siblings—two sisters and a brother. Linda's parents were in their forties when she was born, and in many ways her experiences were that of an only child, since there were fifteen years between Linda and her older sister. A pleasant, agreeable child, she enjoyed playing with her dolls and toys for hours by herself.

She would often join her mother when she had adult guests and everyone would remark on what a delightfully well-mannered little lady she was. Linda's mother seldom found it necessary to physically punish her. A disapproving look or emotional withdrawal would usually achieve the desired effect. Linda's father remarked that Linda always seemed to be harder on herself than either her mother or he could ever be.

Linda adored her father, a quiet, unassuming man who left the running of the household to Linda's mother, a woman of formidable management skills. He was a sales representative for a large company, a position which required that he travel frequently, usually for several weeks at a time. When Linda's father came home for two or three days at a time, he would usually bring a gift for her. His returns were looked forward to with great anticipation by Linda, who basked under his gentle attention during those few special days. Linda's mother considered her husband's attention to their daughter to be too indulgent, but in keeping with the dysfunctional family communication system, did not let him know this in any clear messages.

Linda's mother was a college graduate. She had worked briefly after her graduation but gave up any consideration of a career outside the home when the first child came along a year after she married. It was her dream that Linda have a profession and enjoy the life experiences that she felt she had sacrificed for "duty" and her family. Linda's mother valued propriety and appearance greatly. It was of the utmost importance that her family appear socially "proper."

Sexuality was a topic that was never discussed in the home. "Indelicate" or "shameful" topics were implicitly excluded from family communications. Emotions were to be controlled; losing one's composure was shameful. Above all was the message that life was predictable and safe if one was obedient and followed the rules.

At the age of eight Linda was sexually molested by an elderly bachelor who lived next door. The molestation, a one time occurrence, happened one afternoon after school when Linda accepted his invitation to come over and play with the several cats that he had as pets. Linda's mother had repeatedly warned Linda that the neighbor was "weird" and "funny" and had forbidden her from going near his house.

Linda was quite frightened by her victimizer's strange behavior, but she never mentioned the abuse to anyone and, except for sleep disturbances, exhibited few outward signs of trauma.

Linda had always excelled in school, and she continued to do so. She was a favorite of both students and teachers. Her peers found her pleasant and agreeable but she usually declined any overtures of close friendship. She was regarded as shy and somewhat of a loner.

Linda became a social worker, a career that she has continued in since her marriage at the age of twenty-three. She has done well in her chosen field and holds a supervisory position in a state agency. Linda's husband, two years younger than herself, was her first serious suitor. Linda is the dominant partner in the relationship; most decisions considered of any importance are deferred to her by her husband, who considers Linda to be of a higher social status than himself.

Linda and her husband have recently begun counseling with a family therapist. The identified problems are her husband's inability to hold a job and Linda's inability to express herself emotionally. Anger is especially difficult for her to communicate. There are also many dysfunctional aspects to Linda and her husband's sexual relationship. Linda has phobic responses to being touched in specific ways and recurrent sleep disturbances after any sexual activity with her husband.

Linda remembers the childhood abuse in vague and dreamlike memories that she quickly pushes from her consciousness when they surface. She considers herself to have had a "perfect" childhood. She would like to have children sometime in the future, but worries about the dangers in the world today and the responsibilities of parenting.

THE STORY OF SUSAN

Susan is the only daughter of a respected surgeon in a large west coast city. Her mother, a passive, emotionally dependent woman addicted to alcohol and prescription drugs, was a shadowy, ineffectual figure to Susan as she was growing up.

It was to her father that she looked for validation and companionship. Her childhood and early adulthood were spent fashioning her life and activities around his schedule. Week-ends and vacations were times that Susan and her father always spent together. Susan became proficient in sports — fishing, golfing, horseback riding — and filled the role of the son that her father did not have.

Susan's father never used violence or threats to control her behavior. Rather, she was rewarded for her "loyalty" and "companionship" with material possessions and glowing praise. Susan could do no wrong in her father's eyes. When Susan was eight years old, her father began confiding in her his most intimate thoughts and feelings. He "shared" with Susan the pain, fears, and frustration that he felt about his wife's shortcomings in their marriage. He told her of his stress at work, and he sometimes cried while she held him and comforted him.

By the time she was twelve years old, Susan had replaced her mother, emotionally and sexually, as her father's marital partner. They were constantly together. "Such a close, loving daughter," observers would say with admiration.

Susan's father was a church leader and Susan taught Sunday school. Her mother's addictions remained a family secret. To the outside world she appeared to be a frail individual prone to numerous debilitating illnesses. People held the family in high regard and often remarked about her father's outstanding qualities as a community leader.

Going away to college was anxiety-provoking for both Susan and her father. It was at this time that she began dating, and then it was only when it was necessary for her to have a male escort and her father was not available. It was also at this time that Susan began experiencing problems with the eating disorder of bulimia, gaining and losing large amounts of weight. Unable to experience sexual satisfaction with any person except her father, Susan sublimated her energy and talents into school and preparing for a career in merchandising.

Returning to her home town after college to be near her father, Susan established herself in the community as a competent professional. Her father suffered a debilitating stroke when Susan was thirty, and their sexual relationship was necessarily altered by this. With her father's approval she married a professional associate of his who was twenty years her senior. Susan continued to place her father's wishes ahead of those of her new husband, who made few demands on her except that she be a social asset to him upon necessary occasions. This was an acceptable arrangement for all involved.

At the age of thirty-five Susan continues to be emotionally dependent upon her father and emotionally isolated from other influences. She anxiously guards the secret of their unorthodox liaison and refuses to regard it in any framework of dysfunction. She has convinced herself that if there were any man as worthy as her father she would consider changing some of her behaviors and opinions, but at this time she expresses no belief that this change will ever occur. Susan's eating disorder increased in intensity over the years and now poses a serious threat to her health. She is at the present time using amphetamines in an attempt to lose weight.

SHARED EXPERIENCES

Victims have commonalities, and they are due to the nature of the crime perpetrated against them. Victims are subordinated to the power and control of others. It is tragic that traditional socialization of children plays into the manipulations of the abuser. Children are taught, with the best of intentions, to respect adults. They are given the message in a variety of terms: "Adults know better than children," and "Respect your elders."

Each of the child victims in the preceding stories was used by someone with narcissistic intent. None of the victimizers had any genuine empathy for the child victim. Ann's father used and abused everyone around him. He vented his rage on those most vulnerable to him, his family. Linda's neighbor was fixated on children as sexual objects. It is highly probable that he had molested many other children and was skilled at gaining power over them without the use of physical force. Susan's father set her up, consciously or unconsciously, from early childhood as a surrogate wife. He transferred his emotional distress to Susan and "trained" her to meet his needs.

Ann, Linda, and Susan were all used by someone who was an adult. They were used by someone who took advantage of the nature of a relationship between an adult and a child. Each child was used by someone more powerful and potentially intimidating physically. Each child was used by someone more skilled verbally and intellectually. Each child was used by someone with a more sophisticated understanding of people and life. Each child was used by someone who knew more about her body than she did.

Each child was innocent. Each wanted, as all children do, to be loved, to belong, to be of worth in her parents' eyes. None of the children asked for the abusive encounters. None of the children seduced the adult. Each victimizer was in control of the situation (if not necessarily in control of his own behavior). Each man knew the difference between right and wrong. Each adult was responsible for his offense.

KEEPING THE SECRET

Another commonality of the three women is that of "keeping the secret." None of the women, as a child, experienced any success in efforts to help herself by telling others of the abuse — "breaking the secret." Ann hinted to counselors and friends, but the consequences of telling were too great for her to take the risk of identifying her stepfather. Linda, afraid of "rocking the boat" at home and losing her parents' approval, kept the events of that afternoon with the neighbor to herself. Susan had very little incentive to tell anyone; she feared losing the only "love" relationship she had ever experienced. In addition, she would have been challenging the reputation of a highly respected professional—a religious leader—and all of the people who believed in him. Who would have believed her?

Uninformed victims and non-victims alike often consider the "keeping of the secret" with puzzlement. To understand it better, keep in mind that: (1) at the time of the abuse, the victim is a child; and (2) she is attempting to survive using a child's reasoning and resources. Ann's motives for keeping "the secret" are the most obvious. Her stepfather might have physically injured her, brutalized her mother, molested her siblings or have placed her in an institution if she had revealed the abuse. She was, after all, an identified "problem child" in school. Linda was frightened by her abusive experience with her neighbor and fearful of her parents' disapproval and rejection. She had disobeyed her parents by going to the neighbor's house in the first place. She believed herself responsible for the abuse. Susan's keeping the secret was consistent with her indoctrination since birth—that it was her role to "take care of" her father.

Other women speak out about "the secret."

JOYCE:

In my family you were taught, "You don't tell other people your troubles; You take care of them at home." Don't tell anybody, even grandparents. Nobody knew what the monster was just inside our front door. Everything looked fine. When strangers came in the door, my dad would smile and be charming. When they left, I would get abused again. . . . In school I was shy. When other kids would start to talk about their families, I would just close the door in my mind, or talk about something else, because I wouldn't dare go into what it was like at my house. Because once I began, if I broke the ice, the secret might get out. . .and then there would be hell to pay.

FRAN:

My dad taught me that the secret we had was something special. It was a possession that made us different from other people, so I protected it.

MARIE:

I thought that I was the only person in the world that felt the way that I did. I felt so ashamed inside. So I kept my secret and "acted" normal. I watched other people and did what they did.

The manipulative techniques available to victimizers cover a wide spectrum. They include:

(a) bribes and rewards.

(b) appeals to the child to protect the victimizer.

(c) no verbal message at all, but a non-verbal message that no one will talk about what is happening (what has happened).

(d) shaming messages that it is the child's fault -- that she wanted it as much as the victimizer did

(e) penalties ranging from removal of privileges to physical punishment.

(f) life-threatening statements and gestures.

Victimizers may exploit a child's love of her family in the following ways:

(a) threaten or imply that if the child does not comply, he will abuse other children in the family.

(b) threaten to abuse the mother.

(c) threaten to abandon the family.

(d) threaten to take his own life and/or the lives of other family members.

Overtly or covertly, the victimizer convinces the child to cooperate and participate. The methods of manipulation used by the victimizers in the three stories were not always conscious. They were not always overtly threatening. They were often disguised as "love." They were always a powerful influence on the child and devoid of true empathy.

A final commonality of all our clients, including the three cases we have described, is one which ensures that the "secret" will be kept for many years. It is the emotional deceiver called SHAME.

THE SHAME OF IT ALL

SHAME:
1. The painful emotion arising from the consciousness of something dishonoring, ridiculous or indecorous in one's own conduct or circumstances (or in those of others whose honor or disgrace one regards as one's own), or being in a situation which offends one's sense of modesty or decency. (The Complete Oxford English Dictionary, 1979)

Shame is a chameleon. It is an emotion that often masquerades as humility or guilt.

Humility provides a balance that keeps us from grandiosity—an inflated sense of our own self-importance. When one practices humility she is aware of her own shortcomings while simultaneously loving and respecting herself.

Guilt is the result of engaging in behaviors that a person perceives as being in conflict with her own and society's value systems. It is the result of doing something one believes to be "wrong." Guilt can be resolved through the action of making amends to the person or persons that one has wronged. This might be accomplished through an apology, financial compensation, or a duty performed. Guilt is the result of a behavior and it is resolved, whenever possible, by making amends.

Shame is a sense of being intrinsically worthless or bad. It is not easily resolved, for shame challenges an individual's very essence as a person. It corrodes one's sense of worth as a human being. Shame negates one's sense of personal value quite separate from, and regardless of, one's behavior. It is what a person is experiencing when she consistently puts herself down, when she constantly minimizes her accomplishments, and when she makes statements like the following: "I'm a bad person," or "I feel stupid," or "I'm not good enough," or "I'm just a screw-up."

Shame often lurks behind downcast eyes and a timid or submissive posture. It sometimes cloaks itself with anger, sarcastic humor, or a stoic, defended approach to life. Shame is a cruel and deceptive internal message that says, "I do not deserve success, good people, happiness, or serenity in my life."

Shame is the component of a sexually abusive experience which causes a victim to doubt her self worth. It is hidden in humiliation, demonstrated with embarrassment, and personified by the "feeling" that somehow the abuse was caused by the victim herself. Shame is tightly entwined with a victim's fragile self-esteem.

A 45-year-old mother of three, a recovering victim of incest, describes shame in the following manner:

MARIE:
Shame is the primary ingredient in how a victim behaves and reacts. Shame is a powerful and destructive emotion. It exhibits itself in a variety of ways. It tricks a person into negative and destructive behaviors.

Human beings are not born feeling shameful. Shame is a feeling one person imposes upon another. Anyone who has spent much time around children has observed how susceptible they are to the attitudes of others. A single child in a group will begin to throw a tantrum, and others will quickly follow suit. We observe that children often "pick up," i.e., learn to imitate their parents' attitudes and the attitudes of significant others. Any schoolteacher can give you examples of times when she has entered the classroom in a particular mood, and class members have responded with complementary behaviors.

Children have fragile psychological boundaries. Under the guise of "education" an adult can impose his/her values, emotional responses and beliefs on a child. The imposition of an attitude on a child and a child's resulting behaviors and feelings are examples of how a child can be psychologically abused, of how a child can be shamed. It is in just such a way that a victimizer imposes his shame, the shame of his abusive behavior, onto his victim. As a result, she may feel shame about her physical appearance, her intellect, her abilities, her sexuality, herself. The recovering victim must learn that the shame she feels, or has felt, is not about something "wrong" that she has done; it is about something wrong done to her. She must practice remembering that the shame is not hers; it belongs to the victimizer.

MARIE:

Abuse can take many forms. It might be one incident by a neighbor or it might go on for years with your stepfather. The message to the victim is the same—someway, somehow, YOU are guilty, YOU are responsible, YOU are shameful. You can be shamed with or without words. It can be done with body language and with innuendoes. It can be overt or covert. The words—the shaming message—might have been whispered or yelled or implied, over and over again. It's a rotten deal for the victim, because it's a lie—it's not true at all. But the victim doesn't know that.

At the root of all victimizing is shame. The victimizer believes himself to be bad, worthless, inadequate, a loser—any of the above or all of the above. He may hold a position of respect or authority in the community. He may be highly skilled and competent in his work. He may manage his family with great efficiency. He secretly believes, however, that if people knew the real person he was, they would not like him. The shame is *his* secret.

In the act of abusing a child, the victimizer passes on his shame to the child, just as if it were an invisible and deadly virus. The child feels dirty, bad, and responsible for the abuse. She has been infected with *his* shame. She was not born with it. She was not changed neurologically or genetically by the abuse. She has been influenced by his psychological dysfunction, which manifests itself in the form of shame.

A child begins to feel shameful, to think shameful thoughts, and to believe shameful internal messages as a result of the shaming experiences imposed on her by others. Shame is the result of being victimized. It is passed on using intimidation, humiliation, and/or degradation. It is imposed upon children through ridicule, sarcasm, verbal abuse, physical abuse, emotional neglect and psychological abuse. Childhood sexual abuse is a shaming experience. A vital part of recovery is returning the shame to the victimizer.

THE STORY OF LOUISE

The following narrative is true. It is in the victim's own words. It is a classic and tragic profile of how a child was victimized and shamed.

LOUISE:

I desperately wanted to be like other kids. I wanted my dad to love me, no matter what. My dad would be fine one minute and the next thing I knew he'd slap me across the face. I didn't understand. My dad would hit me if I cried, too, and I didn't want that, so I kept everything inside and pretended that everything was O.K. When he'd take me to the cellar to hit me for the day's "misdeeds," I would look at him and think, "I'm never going to give you the satisfaction of seeing me cry." This was when I was only six years old.

Dad became more violent with his physical abuse as I grew older. When I asked him about the difference between boys and girls, he slapped me around and told me never to ask questions like that again. So I withdrew even more into books and fantasy.

How I hated my father for abusing me and how guilty I felt for hating him. I felt such shame because a child is supposed to love her parents and I didn't all the time. I figured that he must hate me and that I must deserve it. I figured I must be just all bad and no good and no one would ever want me. I would have done anything for his love and acceptance.

Once I climbed on top of the kitchen counter and swallowed most of a bottle of aspirin tablets. What I was thinking at the time was something like this, "If I take these, maybe I'll go away and then they won't have to put up with me anymore." I believed that I wanted to die. I also wanted their attention.

But Dad yelled and hollered at me and beat me. Then I got my stomach pumped and that was painful and scary. We never talked about what I had done or why or anything. Things were still the same only I became even more withdrawn inside myself.

One night when my mom wasn't home my dad came into my room and said that he loved me and would I come into his bedroom for a minute. My heart just about flipped over. He loved me!

I was so happy when he took my hand; I laid down on the bed and so did he. The beer on his breath smelled terrible but it didn't matter. Nothing mattered except that my dad had said that he loved me!

After I laid down he began to gently rub my body. It felt good but also funny—like adult stuff. I was frightened but it felt so good that he was loving me and giving me attention. He put his hand on my chest and I felt such fear, like it just wasn't right. I was so confused; how could something that felt so good be wrong? He put his hand between my legs and told me that he was sorry for hurting me and that this would only hurt for a minute. He put his finger in me and it did hurt for a while yet I still felt loved. My mind was whirling—"Why did I feel so bad?" He was acting gentle and loving, something I had never known from him before.

Afterwards he told me not to tell my mom because it would hurt her and then I would have to leave home. So I promised not to tell. He sent me back to my own room and I cried myself to sleep.

When I awoke the next morning I was terrified that my mom would know that I was different somehow and then I would be in trouble, but nothing was said and everyone acted as if nothing were any different. But my mom seemed angry at me all day.

When my dad came home my mom told him how bad I had been and I got the worst beating I could remember. After that I never felt whole anymore. There was a piece of me that died that night. I can't explain it any better than that.

I felt like I was responsible, somehow. If I hadn't needed my dad's love, approval and acceptance, I wouldn't have done those things with him. If I wasn't so bad I wouldn't need to get love in that way. I hated me more than anyone else and felt alienated from life in general.

Dad came into my bed many times after that, but it didn't affect me like the first time. I saw it as my duty to feel his penis and put it in my mouth. I would feel nauseous afterwards but I felt like I was supposed to do it.

Eventually I lived inside my head and had a fantasy family where things like this didn't happen and I was a good girl and not doing the things I was doing. I would stay in my fantasy for as long as I could. I didn't pee my pants and didn't make him angry.

I quit playing with other kids and just stayed in my head most of the time. The kids on the block thought that I was really weird and left me alone. My foster brothers left me alone, too. They were different than me. They were good and didn't get beat like I did. I felt very apart from them and everyone else. I was like a house that looked O.K. on the outside but was all hollow and phony on the inside.

Louise's abuse was severe. The abuses of power and the shame that she experienced were brutal. She carried "the secret" for many years and, ultimately, was a survivor. The coping mechanism and strategies that Louise used to survive physically and emotionally are typical of those used by many abuse victims. Her story is important because it exemplifies the fact that for a victim to move beyond merely surviving, for her to prevail over the abuse, she must overcome the shame of it all.

3

YOU ARE NOT DEFECTIVE

As a child I felt that I was defective and deserved everything that happened to me. At the same time I protected everyone else in the family. I thought that I was responsible for all of their feelings. CINDY

INTRODUCTION

The previous chapters have shown us that victims are not alone or shameful. This was done by defining terms and concepts, by citing statistics, by presenting the first person testimony of victims, and by sharing our own professional knowledge and experiences together with the experiences of other experts. This chapter will provide additional information to help the reader understand what it means to be a victim. The concepts developed in this chapter are based on the work of psychiatrist Alfred Adler, the founder of the school of Individual Psychology. We will explain why we believe that the experiences of a person's first eight to ten years are an elemental influence on how an individual interprets and responds to the rest of her life. An integral part of this explanation concerns the influences of the family in which an individual is raised—the family of origin.

TO BE HUMAN

A newborn infant is a human being of unknown and unlimited possibilities. She is a wondrous mystery of the universe eager for expres-

sion and fulfillment. Will she develop a talent for music or art? Will she
be a great athlete? Will she find fulfillment as a wife, a scholar, a mother,
a scientist? The possibilities are myriad. It is our belief that every child is
born innocent and perfect.

Innocence is freedom from guilt or shame. It is blamelessness and
lack of worldly experience.

To be perfect is to be complete. Perfection is not something you
can earn or buy. You cannot learn how to be perfect or mature into it.
You are born with it. It is a gift from your Creator. To be born perfect
means that you already have all the necessary parts to be whole. The
potential to experience a full and satisfying life is inside each human being,
waiting to be nurtured into expression. It is that part of one's inner self
referred to by a variety of terms: the creative consciousness, the inner self,
the spirit, the soul.

THE IMPORTANCE OF ENVIRONMENT

*From early infancy onward we all incorporate into our lives the
message(s) we receive concerning our self-worth, or lack of self-worth, and this
sense of value is to be found beneath our actions and feelings as a tangled
network of self-perception.   CHRISTINA BALDWIN*

Imagine that an infant is born with an extraordinary ability to read
and write. The creative part of her brain is more capable than that of the
average person and this talent is apparent from the beginning. Her parents
are supportive, loving and enthusiastic. They expose the child to the best
literature, to stimulating and creative people, and to numerous positive
experiences in which she participates and nourishes her talent. As a result,
the child blossoms. She recognizes and exercises her ability to make a
profound contribution to the literary world. The child experiences great joy
in the expression of her talents — not from a competitive standpoint but as
a creative expression of her inner self.

The most nurturing elements in a child's development are the
opportunities and encouragement to discover and express her capabilities —
creatively, intellectually, emotionally, and spiritually. If she is never

encouraged to believe that she is special, if she is taught instead to assume a subservient role in life, then she may never discover her unique talents or experience the joy of self-fulfillment.

If a child is given the opportunities and encouragement to discover her creative potential, if her environment is conducive to growth and confidence, then she will be free to discover and utilize those qualities which make her the unique individual she was born to be. She will be free to discover and to realize her innocent and perfect self.

Childhood circumstances vary greatly for individuals. There is much variation in the degree to which a child is provided the opportunities and the encouragement to become the person she is capable of being. We often refer to the "discovery of self " or to "the person you were born to be." In both cases it is a reference to a being of wonderful and diverse capabilities. It is a reference to the child that dwells within each of us, calling to be fulfilled—a child born innocent and perfect.

THE CORE BELIEF OF SELF

Perhaps you are wondering, "If every child enters this world innocent and perfect, then why is it that so many people experience themselves as failures, as dumb, or inadequate, or defective in some way? Why is it that so many people have such difficulty accepting the simplest compliment? Why is it that no matter how well some people do in life, no matter how much they achieve, they never really believe that they have done well enough? Why are so many decent and kind people involved in unhealthy relationships with persons who use and/or abuse them?"

It is because a core belief about self is the base from which each person encounters, interprets and responds to her life situations. At the core of all behaviors and attitudes, all triumphs or failures, is what a person believes to be true of herself. What an individual believes to be the truth about her worth, her lovability, and her role in life is the lens through which the entire world is interpreted and experienced.

The foundation of a person's belief system is built upon the lessons taught to her by the important first persons in her life. A child learns who she is and how she is from her primary caretakers—usually her parents, her close relatives, a foster parent, or a parental figure. Virtually all of her fundamental learnings will be taught to her by these important first persons in her life. These lessons come in many forms: parental behaviors that are observed and experienced, and verbal and non-verbal communications.

There will, of course, be other influential persons and circumstances — teachers, friends, clergy, other relatives and acquaintances. These peripheral relationships will make a difference and will be influential in varying degrees. No other relationships, however, will compare in influence to those exerted by her family of origin. Her core beliefs — how she views herself, relationships, and the world — will be a direct reflection of the attitudes and behaviors of her parental role models.

THE STORY OF KATHY AND KRIS

Kathy and Kris are orphaned twin girls who were adopted at birth into two different families. Their stories are composites of the lives of hundreds of infants in hundreds of life situations. We hope to demonstrate how a child's core beliefs are formed by unique and specific life experiences. No individual experiences life as completely good or bad.

We have provided Kris with an "optimal" environment for growth and fulfillment, a home where she is loved and taught to love herself. Kathy has been given an environment without adequate love and nurturance, a home where she is exploited and abused.

Every life experience, in these critical early years of life, is a lesson taught to the child by someone else. Every early life experience is a building block for a child, a foundation stone in the belief system she will build about herself, her relationships and the world. Kris and Kathy have comparable genetic advantages and disadvantages. Environment will determine the differences between their core belief systems. Kathy is adopted into an abusive family system with an alcoholic father, a dependent mother, and no siblings. The other twin, Kris, is adopted into a nurturing family system with a father and mother who share parental responsibilities equally, and no siblings.

EARLY INFLUENCES

With each new day in their respective homes an active learning process is taking place. Within each child a belief system is forming, a belief system from which each child will interpret and respond to her respective world. Even before developing the ability to use language, each infant is developing a unique perspective towards life and the roles she is expected to play in life. At the core of what each child is learning is the most important belief—the belief about her self. Evaluations are being made: Am I good or bad? Am I valuable or worthless? Am I lovable or unlovable? Am I safe or in danger? These questions and many more are processed and reprocessed on a momentary, situational basis.

As an infant in her new home, Kathy begins to cry. No one comes to comfort her or to check for problems. This is a situation which is repeated many times. Children learn through symbols, associations, and/or patterns of experiences. These experiences are the foundation of a belief system.

In her new home, whenever Kris cries someone comes to check on her and to comfort her. She is learning a different lesson than the one that is being taught to Kathy. The infants continue to grow. With each interaction with the world and the people in that world, Kathy and Kris' individual belief systems are becoming more defined. Kathy is often ridiculed and ignored. Kris is consistently given affection, attention, and encouragement. Kris is being taught one thing about her worth. Kathy is learning something else.

The sense of reality that one experiences as an adult is the result of a large repertoire of learned life experiences. Adults have learned that there are resources and experiences available to them outside of their immediate environment. A child, on the other hand, does not have this sophisticated understanding of the world. Her options are limited. She operates with an immature logic. To a dependent child, her home, with its limited number of players, represents the entire world. It is the extent of her reality. Primary caretakers are the most important influences in a child's world. In the first few years of her life a child depends upon her parents for her very existence. They provide the nurturance for her physical and emotional needs. They literally possess over her the power of life and death.

Whenever Kathy is frustrated in meeting her emotional needs, she is given the message that there is something wrong with *her*. Whenever she does not receive the nurturance that she yearns for, she concludes that *she* must be at fault. With each disparaging communication and ridiculing gesture she internalizes the belief that she is shameful and defective. She concludes, "If I was just a little better in school, they would love me." She decides that, "If I just didn't mess up the house so much or fight with Mom, then they would love me."

Kathy is entangled in a painful psychological maze through which she is constantly searching for love and acceptance. She is enmeshed in a pattern of self-defeat. Since she feels herself to be a failure, she looks to others for a sense of self-worth. The people from whom she wants nurturance are incapable or unwilling to provide it. Kathy is learning that she is unlovable, defective, and shameful.

In the other home, Kris is listened to when she is fearful or in pain. Her parents are not overly protective. They guide and support her. She is encouraged in activities she is good at and likes to do. Her self-confidence is nurtured. She is shown affection not only for performing well but just for being herself. She is shown that she belongs and that her presence is a contribution. Her parents instill in her the realization that her sense of value is not dependent upon others. She learns that self-worth and self-esteem grow within her. Through genuine, non-manipulative affection, guidelines, encouragement and nurturance, she develops a sense of her intrinsic worth.

The twins go to school for the first time. During a class time, the teacher becomes angry. She expresses that anger to the class in general. Kathy reacts defensively; she worries that she may have done something to anger the teacher. She doubts herself and withdraws emotionally or acts out in defensive anger. She begins to view school with pessimism and apprehension. Kris witnesses the same event but she interprets it differently. She looks for logical explanations outside of her self. She questions what might be wrong with the teacher. She does not react by doubting herself or her own worth. Kathy's sense of being defective or of little worth is reinforced by this seemingly minor event. For Kris, the event is not a threat to her happiness or her self-worth. If she has questions about the event, she asks her parents for clarification and support, an option unavailable to Kathy.

CONDITIONAL VS. UNCONDITIONAL LOVE

Love is an expression and assertion of self-esteem, a response to one's own values in the person of another. AYN RAND

Kathy's most rewarding family interactions, those most closely resembling nurturing, are experiences with conditions attached. Her father is affectionate when he wants to manipulate and use her. He controls her with fear and intimidation. Kathy has no real choices. Her father has all the power. He is in control. He exploits her needs to meet his own. Her mother treats her with more kindness than her father does, but she often commits similar abuses in more subtle forms. She gives Kathy attention only when she wants something from her in return—to be quiet, to cooperate, to not disturb her father.

Kris' family experiences are quite different. Parental affection and attention do not depend upon performance. Kris is given choices. She is taught to make decisions and exercise control over her own life. Her parents teach her that they are fallible human beings who are doing their best to be good persons and parents. She receives attention, hugs, and encouragement even when she fails. Mistakes are opportunities for learning, and her parents exercise patience and understanding.

Kathy's belief of self is that she is unlovable and of little worth. Her belief is the result of emotional neglect and overt abuse. Kathy is a victim of conditional love.

Kris' belief of self is that she is a valuable and lovable person capable of anything she decides on. It is the result of encouragement, support, opportunities, and unconditional love.

KATHY'S STORY CONTINUES

As Kathy grows up, she witnesses constant and unresolved conflict between her parents. Often her father is intoxicated and physically and emotionally abusive toward Kathy and her mother. Kathy's mother spends most of her energy attempting to placate her husband and not precipitate his angry and abusive behavior. As a young child Kathy retreats to her bedroom and plays with her dolls when her father grows loud and abusive. She fantasizes about living in a family where everyone is happy. As she grows older, Kathy sometimes attempts to "save" her mother by intervening in her parents abusive encounters. When she does this both parents turn on her with anger and disapproval.

More and more often Kathy leaves the house and retreats to the sanctuary of a neighbor's yard. Often it is many hours before she returns home. She is never sure what the atmosphere will be like when she returns home. She learns to go quietly to her room and not "disturb" either parent after violent or unhappy episodes. Kathy's fantasies about living in a happy family become increasingly important for her emotional survival. She carries her fantasy life to school with her and tells her classmates many stories about her idyllic home life.

Kathy's parents are members of a church and sometimes the family attends church together. More often her parents send her to church alone. Her parents speak of honesty, forgiveness, and obedience of God's laws, but Kathy does not observe these concepts demonstrated in their daily living. Often her father misses dinner and comes home late, angry and abusive. Her parents argue constantly about money. Her father controls it; her mother needs it for groceries and other necessities. Her father accuses her mother of wasting "his" money. He does not trust her to handle it responsibly. Kathy's mother lies to her father and hides money from him to maintain the household.

Expression of affection in Kathy's family is distorted. Her father displays affection only when he is in his "scary" moods. He treats her mother roughly when he wants physical intimacy. He is forceful and aggressive. If her mother protests in any way a fight ensues. When her father is drinking, he accuses her mother of being unfaithful to him with other men. He does this in the crudest of terms. Despite her mother's tears and protests, her father will then force her mother into the bedroom and the door will slam shut. Sometimes she hears her mother cry out in pain and her father's voice grow louder and more abusive. Often there will be an ominous silence, which is even more frightening to Kathy. Kathy wanders anxiously about the house unsure of what is happening, fearful for her mother's safety. Once when she gathered the courage to pound on the bedroom door and scream, "Don't hurt my mommy! Please don't hurt her!" her father burst through the door, grabbed her by the arm, and threw her out of the house. Kathy retreated into the comfort of her fantasy world and played with her imaginary friends in the back yard.

Kathy receives many confusing messages about love and sexuality. Sometimes when her mother is not at home and late at night, Kathy's father will be unexpectedly gentle and affectionate with her. Sometimes he will massage her body under her panties or pajamas. This behavior is frightening and confusing to Kathy. Her father usually smells like whiskey and changes moods quickly and without warning. This behavior, like everything else that happens at Kathy's house, is never talked about or explained. Often after a particularly abusive episode, Kathy's father promises that it will never happen again. Kathy does not have much confidence in his promises, even though she wants desperately to believe in them. For Kathy, the core belief of *self* means: unlovable, damaged, of little worth and meeting the needs of others.

KRIS' STORY CONTINUES

Dinner time at Kris' house is a special time for everyone in the family. It is a time when the events of the day are shared. Each family member participates on an equal basis. Kris' experiences and opinions are listened to and respected. Problems do not dominate the conversation. The focus is on sharing the day's accomplishments, special feelings, and new discoveries. Sometimes her mother and father disagree on issues, but seldom is anyone shamed or abused. When there is conflict or disagreement, each parent is willing to apologize. Kris' parents teach her that adults make mistakes too. Everyone's dignity as a human being is respected. Sometimes Kris acts inappropriately at dinner or at another time. When this happens she is grounded or sent to her room until she chooses to behave herself. Kris' parents explain to her why she is reprimanded or punished. She is given the message that she is loved as a person but that some of her behaviors are unacceptable.

Kris' parents strive to live their religious beliefs every day of the week, not just on Sunday. They do not ask Kris to believe what they say, but rather to believe what they do. Kris sees them practicing love and consideration with consistency and honesty.

Kris often sees her parents show gentle affection toward one another. They hold each other and communicate in loving tones. When her mother or father is upset or sad they will touch and comfort each other. Kris' parents occasionally disagree and argue, but Kris does not see them abuse each other physically or emotionally.

Sometimes her mother and father spend time alone in their bedroom. They explain to Kris that everyone needs "private time." They point out to Kris that parents need special times to be alone together just like there are times that Mom and Kris or Dad and Kris spend together. Kris enjoys individual attention from each of her parents. She feels loved and protected by the closeness and safety that her parents communicate to her with their behavior and their attitudes. For Kris, the core belief of *self* means: valuable, lovable and capable of many things.

TWO DIFFERENT BELIEF SYSTEMS

As Kris and Kathy continue to grow, their interactions with people and life become more complex. The perspective that each of the twins brings into adulthood is quite different. Within the boundaries of her individual world, each twin constructs her basic concepts of life. Each formulates beliefs about how they "see" family, love, God, maleness, femaleness, and many other concepts. The pattern of behaviors and attitudes in which each child participates is the system from which she shapes her adult realities — how she believes the world to be. It is the psychological blueprint from which all adult experiences will be interpreted.

(See Illustration 3A.)

ILLUSTRATION 3A

CORE BELIEF SYSTEM PYRAMID

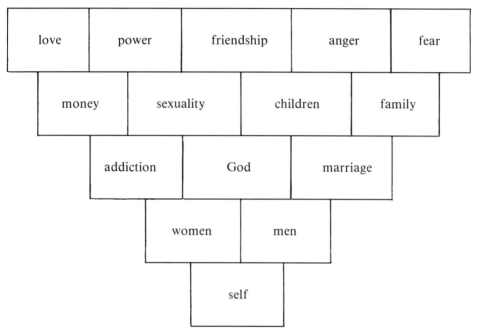

WHO AM I?

A person's core belief system is built upon the concept of *self*. The concept of *self* is the earliest concept in an infant's repertoire. Numerous beliefs — about women, men, addiction, God, marriage, etc. — interconnect to form a core belief about *relationships*. All of these beliefs link together to form a core belief about *the world*. There is no specific order in which beliefs become part of a core belief system. One person's first building blocks might be "women" and "men" while another person would first identify "God" and "family." Each is appropriate for that person. The suggested categories above are usually included in a person's belief system but one is not limited to them. The possible belief categories are as varied and unique as each individual. A place to begin to understand one's adult patterns of attitudes and behaviors is to define the categories outlined above for one's self. Remember that this must be done as the beliefs are perceived through the eyes of a child.

KATHY: RELATIONSHIPS AND THE WORLD

Kathy witnesses a great deal of destructive behavior between her parents. As a result, she integrates strong negative messages about the value of relationships. She learns through observing her parents that men have the power in relationships, that they make and break the rules, that they control the money, that they deliver punishment and rewards, and that their needs are the most important. Kathy observes women as subservient to men and dependent upon them. She learns that women have few rights and no significant emotional needs.

In Kathy's world God is a mystery with little application to real life. She learns the meaning of the concept "hypocrisy" long before she hears the word. Religion is another tool by which people control her with fear, shame, and guilt. In Kathy's world, her father is the supreme being. Kathy hears her parents talk about how God takes care of all His children. Later she watches her parents fight and abuse each other. Her father sneaks into her bedroom and frightens and confuses her by touching her in a sexually abusive manner while talking to her soothingly. She is confused and prays for it to stop. She prays for her mother and father to stop fighting. She prays for her father to not smell like whiskey any more. She prays for him to show affection toward her at times other than when he comes into her room at night. For Kathy, love and forgiveness are terms to mistrust. Hearing that God is all-powerful and all-knowing, Kathy concludes that there is something terribly wrong with her. "Why else would God let this happen?" she asks herself.

Kathy's father's addictions to alcohol and sex are the center of the family's existence. Everyone else's needs are secondary. Money is a way to control people. It is argued over, greedily sought after, and often obtained at the expense of others. Kathy struggles to be more perfect, to please, but it is never enough. None of her efforts gain for her the love and acceptance she so desperately needs. Kathy reacts to the wishes of others. She is incapable of identifying or meeting her own emotional needs. She learns this lesson so well that she despairs that life can be any different for her. She believes that happiness is for others.

For Kathy, her sexual identity is in serving others. Behaviors that her father calls "acts of love" are, in reality, sexual abuse and exploitation. Kathy observes her mother using her sexuality to avoid conflict.

In the abuse Kathy experiences with her father, these messages are communicated: "Your role is to give me pleasure," and "Sex means love." Kathy learns that she can use her sexuality to gain some sense of acceptance and safety with an unpredictable and frightening person. She experiences this distorted "love" as better than abuse. She learns to use her sexuality to gain a sense of control in a "crazy" environment.

For Kathy, the core belief of *relationship* means pain and fear, and the way to experience a sense of control is by using her sexuality. Kathy's core belief of the *world* is that it is unreliable and untrustworthy, a place where other people have fun.

(See Illustration 3B)

KRIS: RELATIONSHIPS AND THE WORLD

Kris learns through first-hand experience and observation of her parents that relationships are places of belonging and safety. She knows that relationships sometimes mean conflict, but that neither relationships nor conflict need to be feared. She has repeatedly observed the beneficial results of working problems through to conclusions that are beneficial for everyone involved.

She is taught that there are no bad emotions. She learns that appropriate anger is a part of being human and that there are times when she has a right to be angry at others and there will be times when others will be angry at her. Anger does not mean that she is less valuable as a person. It is not about her intrinsic value as a human being.

She observes men and women relating on equal grounds. She learns that women can pursue careers and education. She learns that men sometimes fail, just as women do. She observes her father accepting an equal share of traditionally feminine roles—child rearing, household duties and nurturing—without losing dignity or power in his important parental role. Kris observes sexuality as only one dimension of a loving relationship. She is taught that appropriate intimacy is a relationship of mutual respect between persons of equal power. She grows up trusting her own sexuality

ILLUSTRATION 3B

BELIEF SYSTEMS OF KATHY AND KRIS

	KATHY	*KRIS*
SELF	unlovable, damaged, little worth, meet the needs of others	valuable, lovable, capable of almost anything
RELATIONSHIPS (marriage)	frightening, angry, hurtful, men have the power	partnership, safe, belonging, affectionate spiritual
THE WORLD	untrustworthy, for others	opportunities, discoveries
WOMEN	subservient to men, caretakers	equal, achievers, nurturers, power
MEN	powerful intimidating, center of family, everyone meets their needs	fallible, sharing, gentle, strong, nurturing
GOD	controlling, disappointing,	loving, comforting, forgiving
LOVE	sex, pain, exploitation	vulnerability, sharing
SEXUALITY	"love," shame, controlling, meet the needs of others	special, loving, sharing, equality
ADDICTIONS	all-important, pain, fear,	illness, unhealthy
MONEY	men in control, all-important, power	shared, essential but not primary importance
CHILDREN	burdens	special gifts
FAMILY	struggle, pain fear	nurturance, love, support
ANGER	bed, hurtful, not allowed,	part of being human

as a result of never having been sexually exploited by her parents. Money is not used to manipulate or control family members. Kris is often present when budget issues are discussed and her opinion is considered when major financial decisions are made.

Forgiveness and spirituality are concepts which are not only talked about but actualized on a daily basis. When a family member falters or errs, other members are there to love and support him or her. Problems are confronted, apologies are made and offending persons are forgiven. Resentments are not fostered or suppressed; they are confronted and resolved. God is experienced as a loving and forgiving reality who is present in the household on a daily basis. Kris learns to define *relationships* as loving, supportive, and spiritual. She sees the *world* as an exciting place of almost limitless opportunities and discoveries.

LESSONS

Children learn lessons from their life experiences. The messages which are most likely to become internalized as part of a belief system are those which are repeatedly experienced. A child who is occasionally left with a babysitter while her parents go out is not in danger of developing low self-esteem or a fear of abandonment because she has been left in the care of others. However, if a child regularly experiences being left alone or with someone who abuses her, she will learn lessons which foster beliefs of low self-worth. No single incident will necessarily traumatize a child, but consistent and repetitive patterns of behaviors and attitudes experienced by a child will be incorporated into her belief system.

A child who sees her primary caretakers consistently preoccupied with work, substance abuse, or any activity to the exclusion of family functions, learns that these diversionary activities are: (1) more important than she is, (2) more important than children, and (3) more important than the family. A child who observes pornographic materials in the home, hears demeaning jokes about women, and observes her father behaving sexually with women other than his wife learns that women are objects for men's satisfaction, that the human body is shameful, and that marriage is not necessarily a "sacred" institution. A child who is scolded when she innocently exposes parts of her body or touches "her private parts" will learn that parts of her body or even her total sexuality is shameful. A child who is ignored when she asks questions about sexuality learns that such questions are shameful.

Inaction and omission can be as influential as action in a child's learning processes. An example of this is a statement, often expressed by victims, that as children they preferred to be beaten rather than ignored by their parents. The pain of isolation and neglect expressed by so many victims supports the contention that children inherently seek attention and love from their caretakers and will accept it in whatever form it is available. Inadequate or inappropriate love is preferred over no love at all.

The desperate search to be nurtured is observed in almost every sexual abuse victim and may be presupposed in situations where the abuse continues on a long-term basis. For some victims, the intimacy with the parent during the abusive incidents is the closest facsimile to love and affection available to them. The victimizer says the "right" words and may be gentle and encouraging to the victim. In situations where violence accompanies the abuse, a victim may learn that cooperation will save her from even worse abuse.

The "lessons" learned in actions and inactions are both simple and profound, overt and covert. The examples provided here are not definitive. There are many more variables that contribute to each person's core belief system. The belief system established by a child will be as unique as the child herself.

THE SELF-FULFILLING PROPHECY

I look in the mirror through the eyes of the child that was me.
JUDY COLLINS

One of the most observable phenomenon in human behavior is the self-fulfilling prophecy: that which a person believes to be "true" will be made "true" by that person.

A simple example of this phenomenon is an abusive parent who tells a child on a regular basis, "You will never amount to anything!" A child will grow to adulthood experiencing one failure after another, actualizing her belief of low self-worth by dropping out of school, getting in trouble with the law, abusing alcohol, etc. The different behaviors that a person can engage in to fulfill her prophecy are ingenuous and sometimes seem paradoxical, but the results are the same. The belief of self becomes actualized.

A person's beliefs are interconnected in a system; the behavior patterns for fulfilling the beliefs will be consistent with the system and each of its components. For example, the child who believes she "will never amount to anything" will realize her belief in a manner consistent with some or all of her other beliefs. If her family values money highly and despises people of a lower social class she might fulfill her prophecy by dropping out of college and marrying an uneducated manual laborer. If her family values high achievement and marriage, she might fulfill her beliefs of low self-worth by flitting from one job and relationship to another. The ways in which a person can fulfill her beliefs are myriad.

CORE BELIEFS OF VICTIMS

Just as victims of child sexual abuse share many experiences in common, so do they share common characteristics in their core belief systems. There are many factors which influence how each child/woman reacts to her sexually abusive childhood. The child who is the least traumatized by the abuse is the child with an open and supportive family to whom she can go for love and affirmation of her self-worth. On the other end of the continuum, the person who experiences the greatest difficulty is a child from a severely dysfunctional family—a family that is sexually, physically, psychologically or spiritually abusive—that labels her as the problem.

The core beliefs of some of the women who share their lives in the pages of this book are outlined in Illustration 3C.

(See Illustration 3C)

All of these women were traumatized by their abusive childhood experiences. For the victim of childhood sexual abuse, charting her Core Belief System is an important step in her recovery process.

ILLUSTRATION 3C

CORE BELIEFS OF VICTIMS OF CHILDHOOD SEXUAL ABUSE

SELF	RELATIONSHIPS	THE WORLD
BARBARA		
alone, inadequate	painful	everyone else enjoys, not fair
JANE		
to blame, worthless, lonely	hurtful, lonely, uncaring, false, men have power	scary, confusing, nature is pretty, unfair, unlovable
NATALIE		
unlovable	hurtful, false	scary, unfair, lonely
BONNIE		
told pretty, felt ugly, different	money is most important	appearance is important
LOIS		
ugly, lower, two people, stupid, devil's child	painful, superficial, threatening	unfair, place to hide from home, beautiful
BETH		
trade-off, protector, ugly	none except to protect others	for pretty people
TINA		
good, inadequate	forced	unreal
CLAIRE		
at fault, stupid, failure	confusing, angry, ugly	large, animals are friends, frightening
IRENE		
dumb, ugly, nothing right, responsible	sexual, men and women oppose each other	had to be sexual like family
MARIE		
damaged, unlovable, arbitary	winners and losers	painful, scary, unpredictable

CONCLUSION

If you were a victim of childhood sexual abuse, our goal for you is to realize the innocent and perfect child that you were born to be. Part of that process involves recalling your childhood and charting your own Core Belief System.

Examine the first eight to ten years of your life. Do this through the eyes of a child—as if you were two or five or seven years old. Search your memory for what it was like for you at those young ages. Look at childhood photographs in family albums, talk to older family members and friends who were there when you were a child. In a notebook, write down what you learned as a child about important concepts—men, women, love, God, money, etc. There is no special order or content to your Core Beliefs Pyramid. It is as unique as you are. You can build it as high and as detailed as you wish. Construct your own timetable for this project. You may choose to work on it one hour a day or one hour a week. The choice is yours.

When you begin to identify your core beliefs, you will begin to understand ways that you are still handicapped by some of them. You will recognize how some behaviors and attitudes are still active factors in your life today. Identify with honesty and objectivity the ways in which you were hurt by some beliefs and the ways that some beliefs helped you to survive. Identify and consider the ways in which you actualize these beliefs in the present through actions and inactions. Understanding is the key to change. You can choose the concepts that you want to change, the ones that are still causing you problems. You can reinforce and support the concepts that are healthy for you. Trust your feelings about the recall process. Remembering your childhood memories will evoke many emotions. Some will be pleasant. Many will be painful, frightening and confusing. This is a difficult process to undertake by yourself. Ask for help from trusted friends and professionals. If you have a self-help support group that you attend or if you are in therapy, share your memories and insights with these trusted persons.

What you have begun is a blueprint for growth and recovery. You can choose when and how and where you begin this process. Remember that you are in control. Remember that you were born innocent and perfect.

4

YOU ARE NOT CRAZY

It was very difficult and frightening at first, just being here (in the women's group), but now I feel safe here. Just finding out that I wasn't crazy or going crazy was the most important thing I ever learned. LANA

INTRODUCTION

The women victims of sexual abuse that share their lives in the pages of this book are functioning in society with varying degrees of success. A few continue to be enmeshed in dysfunctional behavior and thought patterns, but the great majority have succeeded and often excelled in various life endeavors before or during involvement in educational programs and restorative therapy. To better understand their successes, we must first understand their survival.

COPING:
Adjusting; adapting; successfully meeting a challenge.

COPING MECHANISMS:
All the ways, both conscious and unconscious, that a person uses in adjusting to environmental demands without altering his(her) goals or purposes.

(Authors' note: All of the definitions in this chapter are taken from the *Psychiatric Dictionary,* Fifth Edition, Robert J. Campbell, M.D., Oxford University Press, 1981.)

Every child is intrinsically motivated to seek attention, love, and a sense of belonging or acceptance. In an experience of sexual abuse, a child is thwarted and exploited in her attempts to meet these needs.

How does a child survive sexual abuse when her emotional needs are not being met or are being exploited? How does she keep from giving up, or from going crazy? How does a child survive the psychological terror and physical brutality that often accompany sexual abuse? She does it by employing "coping mechanisms" or "defense mechanisms."

Throughout the text the terms "coping mechanism" and "defense mechanism" will be used interchangeably and regarded as having the same meaning. In this chapter we examine some of the coping/defense mechanisms that abused children use to survive. All defense mechanisms are natural human responses that help us achieve physical and/or emotional survival.

DEFENSE MECHANISMS

When a person puts her hand too near an open flame, a reflex response of jerking the hand back occurs. This is a biologically programmed response which helps the human organism protect itself. Just as persons are equipped to handle physiological trauma like that elicited by the flame, so are they also equipped to cope with trauma evoked by psychological causes.

Sigmund Freud, the founder of psychoanalysis, labeled these mental phenomena "defense mechanisms": Mental attributes which serve to protect a person against danger arising from her impulses or affects. Defense mechanisms are mental exercises in which an individual engages when an action or thought threatens to overwhelm her. If a mother is being verbally assailed by all five of her children at once, she is capable of "screening out" those children's demands which she evaluates to be of lesser importance so that she will "hear" one child's report of a bloody nose. The mother is coping by utilizing a defense mechanism.

The most dramatic uses of defense mechanisms are in the cases of obviously painful traumas. A person who cannot remember a car accident in which a friend was killed is an example of how a defense mechanism is used to avoid psychological pain.

But people use defense mechanisms for coping with more than obvious and dramatic traumas. Any experience which threatens to elicit strong emotional responses such as fear, physical pain, emotional pain, shame, guilt, etc., can activate our mental self-protection systems. A child who is frustrated in meeting her needs for love and acceptance learns to implement coping mechanisms to overcome the pain of that frustration. For many victims, coping mechanisms are survival mechanisms. They may have literally kept her alive and/or saved her sanity.

Defense mechanisms in themselves are neither good nor bad. It is how they are used and the resultant state of mental health or mental illness that determines their positive or negative value for an individual. Coping or defense mechanisms become a problem when a person is persistent or chronic in their usage. A coping mechanism becomes a problem when:

(1) It requires considerably more energy to ignore facts and to avoid realities than it does to face them.

(2) The coping mechanism is used habitually, consciously or unconsciously.

(3) It blocks a person from confronting and resolving stressful experiences that keep her from moving on to new understandings and growth.

In the case of the mother with five demanding children, her defense mechanism of "screening out" will become a problem when:

(1) She finds herself experiencing headaches and other ailments as a result of fending off requests for attentions.

(2) She ignores requests to the point of often being unaware of the children's individual needs.

(3) She is not motivated to learn new parenting skills, problem-solving techniques, or ways to gain parenting assistance from her husband.

For a child experiencing the physical and emotional trauma of sexual abuse, the implementation of a defense mechanism is as natural as withdrawing one's hand from the previously mentioned flame.

In our therapy with adult victims of childhood abuse we have observed seven major defense mechanisms. They are:

(1) Suppression/Denial

(2) Repression

(3) Rationalization

(4) Sublimation

(5) Dissociation

(6) Isolation

(7) Fantasy

To label a pattern of coping as being distinctly one defense mechanism or another is often impossible as well as impractical. The language that clients have used to describe their own experiences is as idiosyncratic and unique as each person's perceptions and vocabulary. It is the norm rather than the exception that persons use more than one method of coping in any one situation.

It is our goal that the seven categories be used as tools by the reader to identify the ways that defense mechanisms enabled her to survive the trauma of childhood sexual abuse.

SUPPRESSION/DENIAL

SUPPRESSION:
The act of consciously inhibiting an impulse, affect, or idea, as in the deliberate attempt to forget something and think no more about it.

DENIAL:
Refusal to admit the reality of, disavowal of the truth of, refusal to acknowledge the presence or existence of (something). . .an attempt to disavow the existence of unpleasant reality.

When someone consciously avoids a reality, she is practicing the coping mechanism called "suppression" or "denial."

LANA:
The way that I stayed "in control" was to not deal emotionally with anything about the abuse. I just decided that it didn't exist, like, "What problem?"

When denying thoughts, feelings, or memories a person is instructing her brain to shut out threatening information.

LOIS:
Because reality was so harsh and painful, I kind of drifted away from it and made up my own reality.

FRAN:
When something came up in my mind about the abuse I would quickly push it away and pretend that it didn't exist.

Most of us know someone who has had a close friend or relative die. When that individual continues to carry on her life as though the person is still alive, she is said to be "in denial." Suppression/denial can serve a useful purpose at appropriate times. It can be helpful for surviving a difficult period in life, and we all use it at some time to some degree. In a healthy person this time of denying the fact that a loved one has died is temporary. The person proceeds through the remaining stages of the grieving process — anger, bargaining, depression and, finally, acceptance. (Elisabeth Kübler-Ross, 1969)

Victims frequently employ suppression/denial as a long-term means of coping with the trauma of sexual abuse. It is common for a victim to "pretend" that a painful event or events did not happen.

CLAIRE:
When I talked about it (the abuse) I was talking about somebody else.

CINDY:
I acted like it didn't bother me or matter to me at all.

There is often a strong incentive to maintain a defense mechanism.

JOYCE:
My dad would hit me if I cried, so I kept everything inside and pretended that everything was O.K. Pretty soon I started believing it.

For some victims the denial involves fabricating early life scenarios as alternatives to the painful truth. The following quote exemplifies how a victim will incorporate denial and fantasy to avoid painful realities.

LOUISE:
I denied all of my past, the whole thing. I painted a make-believe picture in my head. I saw myself as a nice little girl who grew up behind a white picket fence. I never once saw myself as a kid that got placed in a dozen foster homes.

Defense mechanisms require energy, and the psychic price tag to maintain a sophisticated denial system can be high.

JOYCE:

Even when I pretended that it wasn't happening in the daytime,
I would still have these terrible nightmares and wet the bed at night.

LOUISE:

I tried to live in a fantasy world but I couldn't stay there and
I started remembering things. I knew that I must be crazy.

BETH:

I tried to block out the pain and fear because I always had night-
mares over it.

It can be difficult to recognize one's own defense mechanisms. Often they have become automatic and second nature, habituated responses that shield us from pain and fear. We can often discern when someone else is denying reality or failing to take responsibility for her own problems, but identifying our own denials is more difficult and more threatening. Any change, even for the better, is initially experienced as stressful.

To "let go" of defense mechanisms and face the truth can be frightening. We recommend that a person not attempt to do so without competent professional help. It is critical that the defensive behavior pattern be replaced with a positive and nourishing plan for healing and growth. Change requires courage and determination from the individual, competency from the professional helpers, and patience and trust from loved ones.

REPRESSION

REPRESSION:

The (unconscious). . .process of keeping out and ejecting, banishing from consciousness, ideas or impulses that are unacceptable to it.

The mind is comprised of two parts, the conscious and the unconscious. On the conscious level are those memories of which one is aware or has knowledge. The unconscious contains memories not in one's immediate field of awareness. Psychiatrist Carl Jung described the unconscious/subconscious thusly:

> One can perceive, think, feel, remember, decide, and act, unconsciously. . . . How this is possible can best be seen if one imagines the mental functions and contents as resembling a night landscape over which the beam of a searchlight is playing. Whatever appears in this light of perception is conscious; what lies in the darkness beyond is unconscious, although none the less living and effective. (Jung, *Contributions to Analytical Psychology*, 1928)

Repression occurs when a memory is in the subconscious/-unconscious part of the mind. The important difference between repression and suppression/denial is that suppression is a conscious process and repression is an unconscious process.

CINDY:
I went through years when I didn't remember the abuse at all. I was in college and I worked in a school where we had a bunch of kids who had been sexually abused. I had no memories of my own abuse during that time, never once. I had it all blocked out.

Repression is a defense mechanism used by persons experiencing extremely stressful situations. It has been most recently observed in soldiers returning from the Vietnam War. It is the coping mechanism used by a victim of a severe automobile accident who does not remember crawling from the wreckage or seeing the dead body of a companion.

Repression is a common defense mechanism for victims of child abuse. It is the rule rather than the exception when the abuse was severe.

LANA:
I did presentations for the nursing department at the university and for college classes, but I was talking about somebody else,

*other people. I couldn't understand why I felt so emotional about
the subject of child abuse, of any abuse really, any injustice; it
puzzled me.*

Repression as a method of coping can serve a person well and she
may appear to be functioning adequately, even excelling. Outward signs of
dysfunction may not be discernible to the casual observer. There is consid-
erable evidence, however, that symptoms of serious problems can be
present but not obvious in their connection to the trauma. Much like the
veteran who experiences delayed stress syndrome a decade after his combat
trauma, victims of childhood abuse struggle with sleep disturbances, depression, suicidal thoughts, manic behavior, flashbacks, phobic or aversive
reactions, and a variety of relationship and sexual difficulties.

BECKY:
*Whenever anyone would start talking about abuse, I would get very
nervous, and I didn't know why. I would want to "act out"—be
sexual, drink, eat—or do something that would make the pain and
fear go away.*

JOYCE:
*What I remember is a constant feeling of fear . . . I can remember
that the only relief I had from it was when I was in school. School
was one world and home was another.*

It is not unusual for a victim to have repressed memories of
childhood abuse for many years. For some, partial memories are common.
Frequently a victim will compress the memories of several incidents into a
single memory. That is, abuse which happened on many occasions over
several years will be remembered as a single incident. Victims will often
initially report a single incident of abuse.

As they continue in the therapeutic process, other memories will
emerge. Repressed childhood sexual abuse memories are often revealed in
recurring dreams with sexual themes and themes of powerlessness. Some

clients describe visualizing persistent, oblique images during waking hours that appear to have no obvious explanation.

LOUISE:

Nothing really made any sense until I started to remember—to "see" or imagine more experiences. It was like putting together the pieces of a puzzle.

Sometimes these memories are brief images, "flashes" or moments of strong emotional reaction. It is not always the case that a victim's dreams or images are clear and totally accurate memories of her abusive experience(s). What the dreams or images do reflect is a partial "picture" of the unique and personal manner in which she experienced events at a certain age and with the emotional and intellectual resources of that age.

Dreams and images may, at first glance, appear puzzling and of little importance. But if a dream or an image is examined from the point of view of a child's experience, we may discover an experience that was quite powerful, frightening or shaming, and of great significance.

Often one's initial memories are but the tip of an iceberg. Upon first entering therapy, a client often reports a single incident of abuse. As she continues in the therapeutic process, repressed memories emerge. This step in the recovery process can be a period of great anxiety for the client:

MARIE:

I'm afraid that the good feelings that I'm beginning to experience aren't going to last, that I don't deserve to be happy. I'm afraid of the memories that may still come up, afraid that I won't be able to handle them.

You can prepare yourself for memories that may come into the conscious from the unconscious:

(1) The experience of remembering is often frightening. You
may feel "out of control." Ask for help if you begin to fall
back into old thought patterns and behaviors.

(2) It is of the utmost importance that you choose your own
timetable and that you not let anyone decide for you when or
what you will "remember."

(3) Access your network of caring, competent and trusted people
to assist you in your recovery process.

(4) Remember that you are not crazy.

RATIONALIZATION

RATIONALIZATION:
Inventing a reason for an attitude or action, the motive of which
is not recognized. Justification: making a thing appear reasonable when otherwise its irrationality would be evident. Rationalization is the act of, or attempt to, explain to ourselves and to
others that we need not feel the way we do.

As with all defense mechanisms, the use of rationalization is not
always a detrimental intervention in one's life. A need to understand, to
know "why" something is happening, to make sense of it, is a basic psychological need for all persons. Temporarily, momentarily, rationalization can
help a person balance life experiences.

All of us are familiar with times in the past when we have
attempted to "explain away" anger, fear, pain, shame, or another feeling.
We have struggled to get our thoughts and our feelings in balance. Most of
us have had the experience of coming home angry with someone who cut
us off in traffic, or of crying while viewing an emotionally disturbing movie
or television program. We attempted to reason ourselves out of the way
that we were feeling, to explain away our emotional response.

Rationalization becomes problematic when a person attempts to explain away distinct and powerful emotions which require acknowledgment and confrontation before healing and growth can occur.

TINA:
I remember thinking, "Why did he choose me? What did I do to make this happen? This must be why I'm here, for people to do this to."

A battered wife will give as reasons for remaining in an abusive relationship: ". . .because of the children," or ". . .it's my duty as a wife," or ". . .he needs me," or ". . .I love him," or ". . .I couldn't get along without him," or any other of a multitude of rationalizations.

One of the reasons that she remains in distress is because she does not know any other way of coping. Until she chooses, with the help and support of others, to learn and practice new behaviors and attitudes, nothing in the abusive family system is likely to change for the better.

The victim of sexual abuse uses rationalization to avoid the anguish of experiencing difficult emotions and accepting painful truths and realities.

HOLLY:
I wanted to believe that everyone lived the way that my family did, that my dad was just more "friendly" and "emotional" and "touchy-feely" than other dads were.

The sexual abuse of a child is unreasonable and illogical to most people. Few adults understand the dynamics of behavior that motivate someone to molest a child. People respond with shock, discomfort, disgust, anger, fear, and nervous humor. One often hears remarks like, "How could anyone do something like that?" or "I just don't understand that kind of behavior," or "That's disgusting; it's hard to believe that it really happens."

A child, immature and impressionable, is totally unequipped to make an accurate assessment of an abusive experience. Unable to make sense of the abusive experience and looking for a logical and reasonable explanation for what has happened to her, a child resorts to rationalization.

FRAN:
The "secret" made me different from other people, so I decided that this must be the way life was supposed to be—I protected the "secret" and told myself to be proud.

Humor, or at least the facade of humor and its court jester sarcasm, is used by victims to reinforce the denial and rationalization of painful truths.

CINDY:
I hide behind my smart mouth; it's safe there.

JOAN:
I'll do anything to avoid the pain of feeling (memories of the abuse) —usually I joke, laugh, make it sound happy and crazy—you know, like a cartoon.

Humor is also used to achieve the acceptance of others.

JOYCE:
I'm clever—I make jokes about my abusive childhood, make people laugh. I've always been a clown—people love clowns.

When a large part of a child's life is enmeshed in abuse and pain she believes that she cannot risk letting go of her defenses; she cannot risk being vulnerable. She is convinced that she must be defensive to survive.

LANA:
I'm so afraid of being angry, of "losing control," that I always joke and minimize any fear or pain or feeling that I may be experiencing.

GEORGIA:

Whenever any subject begins to feel painful or scary I start joking —
you know, wisecracking, like it doesn't bother me or matter to me at
all. If that doesn't work, I'll intellectualize it. If all else fails, I
just change the subject.   What it's about is trusting, or rather, not
trusting.

One of the greatest tragedies that result from rationalization is that the victim, in her attempt to make sense of her abuse, almost always includes self-shaming messages in her rationalization.

LOUISE:

I felt that I must be responsible somehow. If I wasn't so bad I
wouldn't need to get love in that way. I hated myself more than
anyone else and felt alienated from life in general.

BONNIE:

Everyone told me how wonderful my dad was. So I figured that
there had to be something wrong with me.

If you were a victim of childhood sexual abuse and rationalized your behavior, there are some important messages that you need to recognize as an adult:

(1) You were doing the best that you could as a child to survive in an often hostile and threatening environment.

(2) Your defense mechanisms, including rationalization, kept you alive and functioning at the time of the abuse.

(3) Allow yourself time to learn healthy coping skills to replace old dysfunctional ones.

(4) You will no longer need to rationalize when you become strong enough to face the truth.

SUBLIMATION

SUBLIMATION:
The psychological process of modifying an impulse in such a way as to conform to the demands of society . . . instinctive impulses, instead of requiring control, are deflected into acceptable channels.

Sublimation means putting most of one's emotional energy into a project, activity or role as a means of avoiding experiencing feelings which are stressful, frightening or painful.

LOIS:
I wanted so desperately to be a good person. I had time for every-thing and everyone except me. Somewhere between the P.T.A., church activities and a dozen worthy causes, I got lost.

BECKY:
I had always been a perfectionist in school. When I went back to college it became a driving force in my life that crowded out facing the reality that my marriage was a failure.

Sublimation can be a way to find self-worth through external sources rather than by acknowledging and confronting the inner conflicts which keep one from feeling intrinsic self-worth.

JOAN:
The day I graduated from nursing school was the most important day in my life. My career, helping people, has always been where I have felt most fulfilled. Sometimes I think about marriage and a family, but it's something I just don't have time for right now.

Our culture has traditionally given a lot of encouragement to the man who immerses himself in his work and to the woman who devotes herself to her children. Society is now acknowledging that roles like "work-aholic" and "supermom" are not necessarily healthy ones. They cease to be so when individuals become involved in those roles to the exclusion of dealing with the other dimensions of their lives.

MARIE:

I turned my sexuality off. I poured all my energy into my children. I became a "supermom." But I didn't feel alive. I didn't feel like I ever got to be me. I didn't even know who I was apart from my role as a mother.

A victim's sexuality is almost always a dimension of her life as an adult that has been influenced and sometimes determined by her childhood abuse. Sublimation is a socially acceptable way to avoid intimacy. Sublimation enables a victim to avoid facing fears about sexuality.

LANA:

Everyone else saw the perfect wife and mother—the homemade bread, the hand-sewn clothing, the spotless house. Only my husband saw me too tired to have a sexual relationship except when I was fulfilling my wifely "duty" once a week.

Sometimes a victim will identify with clarity what is going on.

BETH:

I get turned on, like sexual feelings from creating, like drawing and painting and writing instead of by having sex with a person.

Often a victim, utilizing other defense mechanisms such as rationalization and denial, builds a lifetime of sublimated reality.

JOYCE:

My children always come first, before anybody. It's a mother's responsibility to take care of her children, to protect them and meet their needs. I'll never let my kids be hurt by a man the way my mother let me get hurt.

All of the behaviors and goals discussed are admirable when they are in balance with the other parts of a person's life. It is praiseworthy to be a good parent, a disciplined student, a successful business person, an accomplished athlete or an achiever. When these goals are out of proportion to other dimensions of life and exclude loving one's self, they have become unhealthy.

Do you use sublimation as a defense mechanism? Ask yourself the following questions:

(1) Do I usually put other persons' needs (especially my children's or my family's) ahead of my own?

(2) Is saving the world (beginning with stray animals and working up to world peace) a priority involvement for me over cultivating a primary relationship with a partner?

(3) Do I have a dozen worthwhile projects to complete before finding time for myself or for my partner?

(4) Am I usually too tired or too busy to have a sexual relationship with my partner?

(5) Will I work on intimacy with my partner as soon as I have —
  (a) raised my children
  (b) finished college
  (c) been promoted to vice-president
  (d) achieved my financial goals
  (e) lost 10 or 20 or 30 pounds
  (f) run out of excuses

If you answer yes to more than one of the above questions, then we strongly suggest you more closely examine your life. You may be using sublimation to avoid reality and change. Others can point out possibilities to you. Others can offer assistance in the growth process. You alone must decide to reach out and ask for what you need. You are in control.

ISOLATION

ISOLATION:
The separation of an idea or a memory from (the) affective.

AFFECT:
The feeling, emotion or mood that accompanies an idea or a mental representation.

A person remembers seeing her father brutalize her mother on numerous occasions during her childhood. She is able to recount the experiences entirely without affect, that is, any demonstration of feeling or emotion. She is employing the defense mechanism of isolation.

HOLLY:
He just kept hitting her with his fists — in the stomach, in the face, on her breasts. When she fell down on the floor he began kicking her and telling her to stop crying. She was bleeding and it made him real angry when he got some blood on his new jacket.

Frequently isolation is habituated and a person is unaware of how she is utilizing this defense method.

CINDY:
When other women would talk about how they had been abused I would just "blank out" and not hear them. I didn't even know when I was doing it.

TERRY:
I did such a good job of stuffing my feelings that I repressed myself right out of living.

Many times a victim is able to talk about an abusive childhood experience with apparent ease and seemingly little emotional stress.

JOAN:

I can talk about the abuse and act like I'm totally "together," like, "What's the big deal?" I maintain a blank stare, totally detached from any feelings.

A lack of significant affect is sometimes erroneously interpreted as strength. Our clinical experience has been that a lack of affect often indicates a client's need to work through issues left over from the past. A well-defined recovery program and a commitment to therapy are necessary before a person is free of painful memories. Isolating behavior is a problem when it is used persistently to avoid resolving debilitating emotional conflicts.

GEORGIA:

As a victim, I practiced not having any feelings. I kept them hidden so deep inside that even I couldn't find them.

Clients frequently describe the motivation behind isolating behavior as fear. Victims fear what may or does happen if they allow themselves to "feel."

JOYCE:

When I let myself remember what happened, when I feel the pain and fear, I have terrible nightmares.

IRENE:

I'm afraid of letting myself feel, because that's when I get "crazy."

Victims fear losing control.

LOIS:

I was always afraid that I would lose control and become a wild and dangerous person if I had any feelings. So I practiced not feeling anything. I got very good at it.

LANA:

I'm so afraid of losing control, so afraid of feeling, that I minimize any fear or pain or feeling that I have.

Victims express a free-floating anxiety about the feeling of emotion itself.

CINDY:

I'll do anything to avoid the pain of feeling.

Isolating can deceive and confuse a person who uses it as a defense mechanism. A person can mistakenly believe that she is appropriately "in touch" with her feelings. She may be able to feel pain and cry about her abuse, but she feels no anger or outrage about it. Another person may feel anger but is unable to release the pain of the abuse with sadness or tears. To be free to feel means having the ability to spontaneously experience all emotions—joy, fear, pain, guilt, shame, and anger—with equal ease.

There are no morally bad feelings or emotions. Every emotion serves a positive purpose when experienced in appropriate and healthy ways. Total emotional healing occurs when a woman allows herself to experience a wide range of emotions.

There are two significant ways that isolation is used to avoid complete recovery:

(1) A victim will use anger to avoid feeling the pain that is underneath it. If she is filled with anger she will not have room for sadness and pain. A victim may be outraged at the injustice of her abuse. She may cry for another person or animal who has been abused. She may state that she does not need to cry for herself. She may believe that she cannot cry for herself.

(2) A victim will use sadness and pain to avoid feeling anger. Tears and passivity can be so debilitating that she has no

energy left for expressing anger, or she may have been taught that anger is inappropriate.

A person who has been violated and abused has a right to feel the injustice of it all. Righteous anger is strengthening. It enables a victim to heal and to progress in a recovery program. Therapeutic grieving, working through of anger and healing are very difficult processes for the victim who is handicapped by the defense mechanism of isolation.

If you decide that you are using isolation as a defense mechanism, we recommend that you seek professional help to get back "in touch" with your emotions. It is not our goal that a person be totally at the mercy 4of her emotions. Emotions can be misused and abused. There is no benefit in being so emotionally responsive that one is debilitated by feelings of pain, shame, grief, fear, etc. We emphasize equilibrium or balance, a healthy balance between total vulnerability and total detachment. It is our goal that a person be free to feel or not feel, as her choice may be.

DISSOCIATION

DISSOCIATION:
A loss of the usual interrelationships between various groups of mental processes . . . Dissociation and "splitting" are approximately equivalent.

The defense mechanism that we are about to describe is controversial. We encourage the reader to approach it with an open mind. Remember that the following experiences are not reported by all victims of childhood abuse. Do not be alarmed if they initially appear incredulous to you. It is of equal importance that you not be judgmental of yourself or others who do report experiences similar to those described in the following text.

Consistently in our clinical practice victims have described experiencing out-of-body sensations during childhood abuse, and/or a "splitting off" of parts of herself.

MARIE:

One of the ways I coped with the abuse was to escape by leaving my body. My mind, or my spirit, would go up in the corner of the room and watch what was happening, and feel safe.

JANE:

While my dad was sexually abusing me I would be up on a fluffy white cloud listening to music or reading a book or eating chocolates. I could see him way down below me with some little girl that looked like me, and that he thought was me, but I wasn't there.

The function of dissociation for the childhood abuse victim is to block out physical and psychological pain.

BETH:

When the abuse got too painful I would detach and go up into a corner of the room and watch what was happening to someone who looked like me, but it wasn't me, 'cause I couldn't feel anything.

MICHELLE:

When I think that someone is trying to corner me (get close to me emotionally or physically) I get afraid and confused and don't know where I am, or who I am —I just go "away."

There is ample evidence that severe abuse as a child is one of the causal ingredients of multiple personality. We have had several clients that have described phenomena that are consistent with a diagnosis of multiple personality. They were referred to a psychiatrist who specializes in investigating and treating multiple personality behavior. The testimony of these clients is not included in this text.

Multiple personality is popularly referred to as split personality, but it is incorrect to infer from this that multiple personality is identical with schizophrenia. What the women in this text are describing is not, in our opinion, the phenomenon of multiple personality. What our clients are describing is "dissociation," or "splitting." It was a way to survive terrifyingly painful experiences in their early lives. It was a coping mechanism that helped them survive the trauma that usually accompanies severe abuse.

LOUISE:
I felt very apart from everyone around me as a child. I was like a house that looked real on the outside but was hollow and empty on the inside.

LOIS:
I didn't have any control at all. My body wasn't mine. So I didn't stay in it very much.

Dissociation was, and is, used by clients in varying degrees of intensity and frequency.

IRENE:
I "space out" a lot when I get scared, or angry, or just begin to really FEEL something.

Many women generalize the use of dissociation from a traumatic experience with one victimizer to relationships with all men.

CLAIRE:
As soon as a man touches me I just go "dead" and block everything off. It feels like I can't move, like I'm not even "there." The real me is "gone" and just my empty body is left behind.

SEVERE SEXUAL ABUSE

To understand better why a victim would resort to dissociation while experiencing sexual abuse as a child, it is necessary to have some knowledge of what, in our opinion, constitutes "severe sexual abuse." What we share with you now are some of the experiences of women who used dissociation as a defense mechanism against childhood sexual abuse. We will present the testimony of only a few women, but they are representative of many others.

What you are about to read is not pleasant. You may find that reading these stories is difficult for you. It is not our purpose in presenting this information to cause you discomfort. These are true life experiences, experiences that these women lived through. We present them because they are testimony to the courage and tenacity that human beings can exhibit in the face of unspeakable cruelty and abuse.

BETH was sexually abused by both her grandmother and an uncle from the time that she was an infant until she was a teenager. Physically and psychologically, the trauma was severe. She has struggled with and overcome agoraphobia as well as intense distrust of both men and women.

IRENE was sexually and physically abused by her stepfather and his girlfriend for most of her childhood. He often threatened to kill her, her younger sister and her mother if she told anyone. Irene bravely testified against him in court and he is now serving a long prison sentence.

CLAIRE was sexually abused by both her father and grandfather beginning at a very young age. Her brother eventually shot her grandfather when he found him raping Claire. Her grandfather's dead body fell across Claire on the bed. She was eight years old at the time.

MARIE was physically and sexually abused by her stepfather, who began prostituting her to other men when she was eleven years old.

LOIS was sexually and psychologically abused by her father for most of her teen years. Sometimes he would hold a knife to her throat while he was raping her. Other times he would stand in the doorway with a shotgun and threaten to kill her if she ever betrayed him. He often threatened to kill Lois and her mother.

He is currently serving a prison sentence for murdering his brother.

NATALIE's father sexually abused her and sadistically tortured her. He accused her of being a "slut" and a "whore," and gave her many other disparaging, shaming messages.

HOLLY was used in child pornography which included bestiality.

LOUISE was severely abused. Her story was told in Chapter Two.

The list could be much longer, but what you have read is an accurate representation of the experiences that victims of severe abuse have endured. These children survived by utilizing many defense mechanisms, one of which was dissociation. Despite the severity of their abuse, these women are now in recovery.

Many other victims of severe childhood sexual abuse were not as fortunate. It is our belief that a high percentage of the population of mental institutions and many chronically mentally ill persons were victims of severe childhood sexual abuse. Victims who, unable to overcome the trauma of the abuse, coped by successfully dissociating from the reality of this world for another, less painful one.

In the recovery program outlined in this book, victims who used dissociation to cope with childhood sexual abuse will learn that:

(1) You were not crazy when you used dissociation to cope with your abuse.

(2) As a child, dissociation helped you to survive.

(3) As an adult, you can learn to replace dissociation with other, healthier behaviors.

FANTASY

FANTASY (PHANTASY LIFE):
Daydreaming in contradistinction to thinking that is logical and realistic . . . phantasy life gives the illusion that wishes and aspirations have been fulfilled; it thinks obstacles away; it transforms impossibilities into possibilities and realities . . . it is a search for pleasurable representations and an avoidance of everything likely to cause pain.

Next to dissociation, fantasy is the defense mechanism most likely to convince its user that she is "crazy." It is important to recognize that the use of fantasy as a defense mechanism does not identify the user as psychotic. The women in this book who used fantasy as a defense mechanism were not psychotic; they were not crazy. They were coping with their abuse.

JOYCE:
Because reality was so harsh and painful, I kind of drifted away from it and made up my own reality.

Of all the defense mechanisms, fantasy offers the greatest comfort, moments of peace, contentment and security to the abused child. In the fantasy life a victim is able, for varying periods of time, to experience what she believes is a "normal" life style.

LORRI:
When I would go out on a date with a guy, I would pretend that he was "Mr. Perfect." I would see the "love" in his eyes, how he thought that I was someone special, and how he was going to love me forever.

ANDREA:
I used to pray for my real dad to come and rescue me from my stepfather. I just knew that if I believed hard enough that he would, someday. I pretended that he and I would live together

*and be very happy. I daydreamed about it all the time, imagining
how I would arrange the furniture in our home, what meals I would
cook for him. It was very real to me, and very comforting.*

Fantasy can range from relatively simple "wishing" to the fabrica-
tion of elaborate life scenarios. Fantasy gives a victim hope.

LORRI:

*I used to wait by the window at the (juvenile) detention center
believing that my dad would come along and take me back home.
You know, I fantasized he would come in and be all happy to see
me, and apologize for all the things that had happened. And Mom
would be all strong and ready to help. I don't know how many
times I waited at that window. I know a lot of the girls there gave
me a hard time about it.*

The distinction between one defense mechanism and another is
frequently difficult to discriminate. The construction of alternative
life scripts often accompanies the suppression, denial, or repression
of memories.

JEAN:

*I used to tell people that my father was dead, that he had been
killed in the war. Everyone thought that he was a hero. After
awhile, I began to believe it, too.*

Marie's story exemplifies the fact that the traditionally defined line
between "sanity" and "insanity" may be quite blurred for someone experiencing sustained abuse.

MARIE:

*I dealt with all this (abuse) by living in a fantasy world. School
became my safe place and books became my reality. I escaped into
another world and it was in the books. I thought also, at the same
time, that I was probably insane.*

It makes perfect sense that victims sometimes lose track of the so-called "real world."

JANE:

I have no concept of what reality is. When I tell my dad all the stuff I've started remembering, he denies it or doesn't remember it.

There is always the possibility that a victim who consistently and persistently utilizes psychological defense systems, particularly fantasy, to survive, may not "come back" from their alternative reality.

MARIE:

I used to hide from my stepfather in the cemetery that was up on a hill near our house. I chose a grave that felt safe to me and many times I would sleep there all night. After awhile I developed a relationship with the person who was buried there. He had been a soldier in the Civil War and he was very gentle, kind and under-standing. I believed that he would always take care of me and keep me safe. I loved him dearly and, for me, he was very much alive.

Marie was one of the fortunate ones. She was intelligent, resourceful and determined to survive her abuse. After many years of therapy and the loving support of therapists, family, and friends, she has prevailed. There will always be struggles; old wounds will ache sometimes and old fears will surface, but she has discovered her path to recovery, and she is following it. She has an excellent chance of maintaining her healing process and continuing to grow.

If a victim habitually used fantasy as a defense mechanism as a child, this will be detrimental to her as an adult if:

(1) She continues to live in denial and in a make-believe reality. (So much energy will be expended to maintain the fantasy that "real" self-fulfillment will probably elude her.)

(2) She evaluates herself as "crazy" because of her use of fantasy life or fantasy as a child and she allows the resultant shaming of herself to hold her back from growing and healing.

Remember Louise's story. Until she moved from the perceived safety of her fantasy world to accepting the painful reality of her abuse, she was in debilitating psychic conflict.

LOUISE:

I denied all of my past, the whole thing. I painted a make-believe picture in my head. I saw myself as a nice little girl who grew up behind a white picket fence. I never once saw myself as the kid that got placed in a million foster homes. I tried to live out that fantasy life and I couldn't do it. I started remembering things. Nothing really fit together until I started remembering things — it was like putting together the pieces of a puzzle.

The pain of facing the truth about childhood sexual abuse cannot be avoided. It is comparable to the pain that a person experiences after undergoing a needed surgical procedure. It is the pain of healing.

If you were a victim who used fantasy to cope with your abuse as a child:

(1) You lack confidence in your own sense of "reality."

(2) Regularly check out your sense of reality. Ask, "Do you understand me?" Ask, "Am I making sense?"

(3) Seek out persons who understand you, to whom you "make sense."

(4) You will have many questions which follow the general pattern of "Does anyone else see or feel what I feel?"

(5) Participation in a self-help support group with other recovering victims can be invaluable in validating your recovery process.

(6) Your questions and doubts are appropriate and sensible. They will help you build an accurate sense of reality and confidence in your own perceptions.

CONCLUSION

Defense mechanisms are the tools that persons utilize in response to rigorous and challenging life situations. Defense mechanisms have enabled abused children to endure psychological and physiological neglect and brutalization. Because many persons used coping mechanisms to survive, their lives and sanity were preserved. Some persons coped by letting go of their "sanity," by choosing "insanity," and sometimes, even death.

Understanding the adult use of defense mechanisms serves a vital purpose for victims of childhood sexual abuse. The habitual use of defense mechanisms enables a victim to avoid emotional pain, i.e., "feeling." It does not provide long-term resolution for traumatic problems. Childhood sexual abuse manifests itself in a victim's life in a variety of ways — psychosomatic illnesses, sleep disturbances, phobias, free-floating anxieties, sexual dysfunctions, generalized emotional pain, etc. The handicaps a victim experiences physically and mentally will continue with varying degrees of intensity until the causal issues are acknowledged, dealt with, and put into perspective with the rest of her life experiences.

It is relatively easy to identify when someone else is failing to take responsibility for her own behavior, to recognize when another person is denying or avoiding reality. It is far more difficult for an individual to identify her own coping mechanisms and recognize when she is using them. As a child, defense mechanisms are implemented without sophisticated understanding of one's own psychological functioning. They frequently become patterns of behavior that are outside of conscious thought, and thereby elude one's awareness.

Speaking with someone who has lived in a large city all of her life might elicit a remark as to how incomprehensible it would be for her to consider living in the wide-open spaces of Montana. Conversely, someone from Montana might regard existing within the confines of city skyscrapers as totally unacceptable. Neither person is wrong. What has become "reality" for each person is that which she is most familiar with as a result of early life experiences. The manner in which each person acts out her life script is shaped by the dimensions of her environment, and that which is "natural" and familiar to each person is unique. To step away from one's established patterns of living is difficult.

To relinquish familiar methods of coping and to face new realities can be frightening. It requires courage, sometimes the assistance of professionals, and the support of loved ones. Like moving from the city to the country or vice versa, moving away from a preferred method of coping, even when the move is beneficial, is like losing an old friend. It means facing the fear of the unknown. It requires filling the gap left by that loss with productive and healthy new behaviors and attitudes.

Stress responses are common. There may be fear, headaches, bodyaches, anxiety attacks, tears and a variety of stressful responses. Emotional pain accompanies psychological growth and healing. Human nature being what it is, identifying and "owning" one's own behavior and attitudes eludes most of us until a crisis forces us to take a look at ourselves.

The Chinese have a symbol for the word "crisis." It is represented by the horns of an ox or a water buffalo. One horn symbolizes "opportunity" and the other symbolizes "danger." When faced with a crisis, it is up to each of us as to which horn we choose.

To the recovering victim of childhood sexual abuse:

(1) The defense mechanisms that you used to survive childhood sexual abuse were necessary at that time in your life. You were not shameful for using them. To believe that you were shameful is a trick of the victimizer. The shame belongs to him.

(2) Be patient with yourself. Do not expect to be quickly free of lifelong patterns of coping and do not expect to release them without pain and effort.

(3) Be gentle with yourself. There are many similarities in victims' experiences, but each woman's journey to recovery is also uniquely her own.

(4) As an adult you can acquire new behaviors and attitudes, ones that will facilitate healing and growth.

(5) There will be many moments of joy as you discover yourself in your recovery program. Celebrate each victory, however small it may be. It is a triumph of optimism over despair, of pride over shame.

(6) Ask for what you need.

(7) You are in control.

5

PREDICTABILITY, CONTROL, AND POWER

My stepfather was constantly masturbating me, stimulating me from the time that I was three years old. But he taught me that I was not to touch myself or he would punish me severely. I believed him because he did punish me often. So I didn't touch myself. I didn't have any control at all. My body wasn't mine. So I didn't stay in it very much. MARIE

INTRODUCTION

In the late 1960's Martin Seligman and his associates conducted research into what was termed "learned helplessness." In their experiments with animals, he found that those which experienced randomly timed, inescapable events, such as electric shocks, would become passive receivers of the shocks. They gave up and learned to be "helpless." They lost the motivation to escape and, instead, endured. Seligman and his group also discovered remarkably similar behavior patterns in human subjects who experienced inescapable loud noises. Over the years following, researchers in this area of study further demonstrated impressive correlations between learned helplessness and the phenomenon called depression.

The work of Seligman and his contemporaries is important to recovering victims of sexual abuse in the two following ways: (1) Subjects who can predict impending unpleasant experiences suffer less stress than whose who cannot predict such events. (2) Subjects who can control to some degree the impending unpleasant experiences suffer less stress than those with no control.

PREDICTABILITY:

(The quality of being able) to foretell or declare in advance; (to) foretell on the basis of observation, experience or scientific reason.

CONTROL:

(verb) to exercise restraining or directing influence over. . .to have power over.

CONTROL:

(noun) power or authority. . .(also) direction, regulation and coordination. . .(also) a mechanism used to regulate or guide the operation of a machine, apparatus, or system. *(Webster New Collegiate Dictionary, 1975)*

Human beings need to believe that there is order to their lives, that there are laws of cause and effect by which to understand, foretell, and influence the events of life. Without predictability and the resulting sense of control, one experiences stress in the form of physical ailments and psychological disorders.

In Chowchilla, California, in 1976, twenty-six children on a school bus were kidnapped and held for twenty-seven hours against their wills. For sixteen hours of that time, they were in a truck-trailer buried underground. None of the children were sexually or physically abused. For those critical hours, however, their lives were in someone else's hands.

Lenore Terr, M.D., did a follow-up study of the children four years after that fateful event. Doctor Terr noted that the children persisted in the thought that had they done something different, then they would not have had to experience the trauma of the kidnapping. Many of the children revealed this in attempts to identify what they had done to bring the "bad luck." Some tried to identify indicators of the impending trauma that they should have recognized. Some blamed their parents for not having anticipated the kidnapping. Weeks and months later, when recalling the events of that day, the children sometimes distorted the sequences of events in their attempts to explain how they should have anticipated the crisis. Dr. Terr concluded, "In a sense, the child chooses personal responsibility and even guilt for the event over utter helplessness and randomness."

THE NEED FOR PREDICTABILITY AND CONTROL

There is a basic human motivation to observe and identify patterns of events so that life may be perceived as predictable. If life appears predictable, then it can be controlled to some degree and one's stress level minimized under adverse circumstances. In the absence of a more mature understanding of life, a child will tend to take personal responsibility for traumatic events she experienced that were actually caused by factors separate from, and even unrelated to, her existence. She thereby maintains the belief that she has control.

Victims of childhood sexual abuse and dysfunctional families have just as much, if not more, need for predictability and control as anyone else. In a victim's world, the family of origin is often replete with unhealthy relationships, confused communications, and a general shame orientation. For her, the dysfunctions become predictable. She learns to have a sense of control in unhealthy interactions. The shame directed at her reinforces her natural tendency to assume responsibility for the painful incidences in her life, and reinforces her negative core beliefs.

RUTH:
I never knew when my dad was going to get angry, so I would make him angry just to get it over with.

LOIS:
I could control my dad by crying. It would mellow him out, make him stop hurting me. It didn't stop him, but it did make him stop hurting me and that was better than being both sexual and being hit.

Years of living in this scenario set up the victim for a lifetime of self-defeat, because it is the life of dysfunctional relationships, poor self-esteem, and near helplessness which becomes most familiar to her. She developed a belief system which perpetuates her struggles. Those relationships or life situations which do not fit her experience of predictability, she misses.

The victim is attracted to those life patterns which are most familiar, that is, the life patterns with "rules" similar to those she grew up with, the ones she learned in her family of origin. She is attracted to experiences and patterns that fit within her belief system thereby confirming her sense of "reality." She copes with stress in the same ways she did as a child. She utilizes the defense mechanisms that served her then. She interprets current relationships through her early experiences. She meets her present emotional needs with the strategies of the past.

Everyone has had the experience of being "out of one's element," of having to cope in a situation which was unfamiliar. Perhaps it was an elegant dinner party with unknown rules of etiquette. Perhaps it was a date with someone from a different lifestyle or culture. In either case, the situation was one of unfamiliarity. The rules for appropriate behavior were foreign. In such situations a person might have felt disoriented, out of place, highly self-conscious, or frightened. Life circumstances which are unfamiliar will produce some level of stress response. The natural tendency is, therefore, to spend most of our lives staying close to the familiar so that life appears predictable and within our control.

ALTHEA AND CHERI

There is great variety in the nature and degree of predictability that each individual requires. Consider the examples of Althea and Cheri. Althea is a thirty-year-old woman who has worked on the same assembly line job for ten years. She derives great security from the fact that she has lived in the same house for her entire adult life. She knows her work and vacation schedule for weeks or months in advance . She only participates in events that she has scheduled ahead of time. Althea is an example of a person who prefers a lifestyle with highly structured schedules and plans.

Cheri is a thirty-year-old woman who travels around the world. She avoids being involved in any serious personal commitment. She meets financial obligations in a haphazard and erratic manner, seldom knowing where she will be or with whom she will be traveling from week to week. She expresses little concern about her plans for the future, whether they be for next week or next year. Cheri is an example of a person who prefers a lifestyle with no schedules or formal plans.

Althea grew up in a family where daily and monthly schedules provided security and rewards. This lifestyle allows her to raise her family with the same security and familiarity. It is also true that Althea does not possess the psychological resources to manage a lifestyle with more options or spontaneity. Cheri grew up in a home wealthy in money but poor in loving, dependable relationships. She is confident and autonomous, living by her wits, a style she developed as a child. It is also true that commitment and relationships frighten her; she has not developed the internal strengths to commit to either. Some of their beliefs are apparent to Althea and Cheri; many of their beliefs influence them from outside of their awareness. For both Althea and Cheri, life is predictable. Each woman is living a lifestyle based on her established belief system. Each uses her learned methods of controlling life and the relationships therein.

While Althea and Cheri differ greatly in the style in which they fulfill their needs, they are similar in two important respects: (1) Both women have predictability and control in their lives, and (2) Both women experience predictability and control in correspondence with the belief systems each formed early in life. Each woman has created a reality that conforms to the beliefs and resulting expectations she developed as a child.

LEARNING CONTROL

Childhood abuse is an abuse of control. The child victim has few choices and, in an attempt to increase predictability, learns to control situations to whatever degree possible and by whatever means available. As mentioned earlier, these learned patterns of control can be carried through adolescence and into adulthood.

Two avenues through which a victim can increase her sense of control and thereby decrease the stress of an abusive experience are: (1) internally, by utilizing defense mechanisms, and (2) externally, by exercising control of her physical environment.

INTERNAL CONTROL

As reality becomes more threatening, the victim's mind alters her mental experience of reality. She may suppress or repress memories. She may isolate in order not to feel so intensely. She may distort the sequences of events in recalling them. Although the external circumstances are unchanged, the internal experience of those circumstances is changed through the conscious or unconscious use of defense mechanisms.

The natural process of internally controlling the experience of abuse through the use of defense mechanisms is a process which frustrates recovering victims. In recounting to others what happened to them, they sometimes contradict themselves or confuse the order of events. Elapsed time during or between experiences may be distorted. Friends or family may disagree with facts presented. Besides the fact that the victim may alter memories in order to psychologically protect herself, friends and family may also relate distorted perceptions of events out of fear, shame, or denial. The result is that the exact details of abuse experiences can be difficult to ascertain.

Nowhere is this dynamic more frustrating than in the court of law. The use of defense mechanisms works to the favor of the offender in the prosecution of sexual abuse cases. In court, evidence is the foundation of any case. In sexual abuse cases, often the primary evidence is the testimony of the child. If the child recounts the events of abuse inconsistently or in a manner incompatible with other evidence, then the child's testimony is attacked by the defense as being false. The defense suggests that the child was engaging in fantasy or was recounting a story prompted by an adult. It is true that there are an increasing number of questionable reports of sexual abuse. However, to rule all those cases of tenuous child testimony as mere fantasy or as a result of prompting by an adult is an error.

The internal altering of an experience through defense mechanisms is a natural result of a psychological threat. This, combined with the fact that children go through varied developmental stages in which they have a range of abilities to conceptualize reality, makes the chances of proving cases of abuse immensely difficult — not because children lie, but due to the nature of the human mind and due to the requirements of the judicial process.

When memories start to come back, they may be dreamlike. Often the memories do not appear to make sense with other facts that a victim remembers. Numerous experiences may be condensed to a single event. The location or person involved may be unclear. The victim may be confused and frightened. It is not because she is lying or is crazy. It is more likely that she has coped with the facts by using her internal means of control — her defense mechanisms.

EXTERNAL CONTROL

A victim can decrease her stress by exercising control externally. She may manipulate, to some degree, the timing of the abuse, the circumstances in which it occurs, or the person involved. She may find that the abuser is in a better mood at certain times of day. She may find that being "sexual" gains her favors. She may discover that the presence of other people in the house decreases the probability of abuse, and so she manipulates others to keep them in the house. All of these are examples of coping. All are strategies which serve the child by increasing her real or perceived control. All can be carried into adulthood as habitualized patterns of controlling.

MARIE:
My father was a very physically abusive man and very unpredictable. I learned to always wait and find out what mood he was in and then adapt my mood to his. I still do that with men today. I always try to get in what feels like a "safe" position.

For moments, hours, or years, Marie was manipulated in covert and overt ways. She was not free to experience and express the uniqueness of the person she was born to be, a child of creativity, enthusiasm, and innocence. To survive, she had to conform, please, or fight. She had to repress her "true self" to minimize the neglect and abuse. Experiences of helplessness and powerlessness brought with them the feelings of pain and shame.

An abuse victim, as a result of the manner in which she is forced to cope, becomes a reactor. She learns to control through indirect means.

She grows up in a system which forces her to adjust her behavior in order to minimize her pain. She learns to influence the timing and circumstances of abuse when she cannot avoid it. She may be sexually provocative in an attempt to gain control of relationships, this being the unconscious strategy she was taught. Her patterns of control were necessary. They enabled her to cope.

> *JOYCE:*
> *I learned to perform for him. "Perform" is the right word, act, use the power to survive. I learned to be a good actress. Because if I didn't, the stakes were survival.*

> *LANA:*
> *I try to control the people in my life rather than controlling myself.*

One of the myths of sexual abuse is that a child who is achieving in school must be doing well at home. Another version of this myth is that the identified abused child doing well in school is in recovery. She may be improving, but it is not necessarily true that she is recovered or that home is now functional. School is often a place of physical safety and a source of emotional nourishment, a haven from the painful reality of an abusive home environment. By gaining a sense of worth in school, she decreases the pain experienced at home and increases the control experienced internally.

> *RUTH:*
> *I got hit for crying. I could control my father by being very, very good and getting good grades, by being "perfect."*

Ruth was caught in a web of tragically deceiving herself and deceiving others. As long as she appeared "perfect," her stress was minimized. She grew up striving endlessly to meet her abuser's idea of perfection. She tried to wear perfect fashions, to apply perfect make-up, to develop perfect intellect, and to never conflict with anyone in her life. She became accomplished in this role and was highly regarded by all those who knew her. The tragedy was that no matter how hard she strived, she never felt "good enough." She felt that she was constantly on the edge of being "out-of-control." She never allowed herself to get close to anyone, her two marriages failed, and her businesses never quite "took off." Underneath all the "perfection" was an empty, frightened, person who did not truly believe any part of her perfection.

For victims, being caught off-guard can be terrifying. Surprises are despised because victims grow up under circumstances in which the unpredicted is frightening or shaming. Keeping the victimizer off-guard was to her advantage — she had more control. When she could not dissuade him or avoid the occurrence of the abuse, she could sometimes influence the circumstances under which the abuse occurred, adding control and predictability.

JOYCE:
He'd hug me and if I didn't hug him back in just the right way, he'd get mean and hurtful. So I learned real fast how to keep him happy. I ended up being two-faced about everything. Just to be sure there would always be a way to escape.

MARIE:
My father was a very brutal person. I could sense when the storm was coming. So I knew that in order to keep the storm away, I had to behave in certain ways. So I learned to almost automatically start doing things to please him — to try to keep the storm away. If I could see that I couldn't keep the storm away, I'd just provoke him in order to get it over with.

To survive, maintain sanity, or increase her sense of control, the victim had to become highly sensitized to the victimizer. She learned to watch him very carefully and be alert to subtleties of behavior. She tailored her behavior to meet his moods and maximize her effectiveness in dealing with him. She learned to anticipate every possible outcome of a situation. She rehearsed in her mind all the different possible alternatives for handling a situation and what the results of each might be. For a five or ten-year-old, this was not a conscious plot to dominate the family or overthrow her father. These are learned behavior patterns which are the natural result of coping with abusive power.

NEW FAMILIARITIES

A victim of childhood sexual abuse must resolve the emotional traumas of her past and learn new methods of control. Until then, she is doomed to reenact previous dysfunctional life situations—the same roles, the same counterproductive patterns of "control," and the same emotional consequences.

It is difficult for persons who have not been abused to understand why many adult women who are capable in other areas of their lives remain in relationships which are abusive. In frustration, they often conclude that the abused woman must like being abused or she would do "something" to escape. The truth is that most women in abusive life situations are there because they lack the psychological, physical, or economic resources to make major life changes. The predictability of their present situations is less frightening than the unpredictable alternatives. The "reality" of the present situation is consistent with the reality of their families of origin and their resulting belief systems. Until the pain, frustration, or fear of life as it is becomes greater than the fear or pain of entering into the unfamiliar, they will remain stuck in the past. It is "reality." It is familiar. It is consistent with what they believe of themselves, relationships, and the world. They do not know or believe that it can be any other way.

The victims of sexual abuse and dysfunctional families have to embrace the unfamiliar in recovery. In order to build a healthy belief system with "new rules" for predictability and control, new and unfamiliar life experiences are necessary. A victim must develop a new sense of reality in which she can trust. Victims are used to family systems with secrets, shame, manipulation, and denial. To grow, they must cultivate relationships of openness, sharing, and honesty.

Victims were taught to protect those persons in their childhood who failed them. They were taught that this was "love." Now they must practice accepting and assigning responsibility where it belongs. Victims are familiar with relationships of distrust and disappointment. In health, they practice fighting for and accepting faith, trust, and happiness. Abuse victims are used to relationships with two realities: the facade and the truth underneath which is never spoken. Transparency is the goal of persons dedicated to growth—"What you see is what you get." Those who believe themselves to be powerless accept as their destiny negative beliefs of self. Women of power learn to recognize this deception, confront anyone who seeks to perpetuate it (themselves included), and declare their commitments to success and health.

THREE FACES OF FEAR

A primary step in recovery is learning to identify and distinguish between different types of fear responses. There are three types of fear that a victim needs to be aware of and to practice identifying. Each can be identified by the response it evokes within the individual.

HEALTHY FEAR

Healthy fear motivates decisions and behaviors which insure personal safety. Healthy fear reflects an accurate assessment of a situation and the psychological and physical dangers present. It is an innate warning system which tells an individual to protect herself and her loved ones. Healthy fear results in self-preserving action. It warns a woman that she is in a potentially dangerous situation, that the person she is with is unhealthy for her, or that she needs to take action to protect those she loves. From this type of fear comes wisdom. It reinforces and is drawn from healthy opinions of self, relationships, and the world. It carries the message, "If I love myself, I take care of myself."

Some examples of healthy fear are as follows:

(1) The woman who is afraid of her new boyfriend's inappropriate advances toward her teenage daughter.

(2) The woman who fears being involved with a partner whose unpredictable behavior includes violence towards himself and

others or whose mood swings range erratically from euphoric happiness to sullen rage.

(3) The woman who fears being physically intimate with a partner who hurts her emotionally and physically during the sexual act.

ATTRACTION-TO-DANGER FEAR

This fear results in self-defeating or self-destructive actions or inactions. It requires denial and delusion. It relies on negative beliefs of self and relationships. A woman in this situation finds herself irrationally drawn towards an object of fear, usually against her better judgment. People around her advise her against her actions and she may even ask herself at times, "Why am I doing this?" Often she is unaware of, or may deny, the degree of fear she is experiencing. She may, in fact, experience an accompanying decrease in feeling altogether. As she gets closer to the familiar object of fear, old coping mechanisms are activated and she begins to cut off her emotions, to isolate, or to use other coping mechanisms which have become habitualized.

She is moving into a self-defeating and self-destructive pattern. Despite the fact that she may know better, she keeps going back to familiar relationships, familiar abuses, familiar pains and fears. The fear and accompanying emotional pains are "old friends." She may embrace the experiences with the delusion that "it is her lot in life." She feels out of control, but the pattern she is in is, in actuality, controlled and predictable. It is a familiar pattern.

The object of fear is not always a person or a relationship. It can be particular scenarios of life events. Whatever the specifics of the fear situations, she experiences an alluring attraction to them. It is an attraction to behavior patterns connected to unresolved past experiences. It also serves the function of fulfilling negative beliefs of self, relationships, and the world. It carries the message, "If I am of little worth, then I do not take care of myself or experience serenity."

Some examples of attraction-to-danger are as follows:

(1) The woman who is repeatedly involved with forceful and unstable men, physically abusive men, drug users, or alcoholics.

(2) The woman persistently drawn to dangerous activities and is constantly flirting with death or serious injury.

(3) The woman who constantly is involved in dangerous life situations in order to "save" people or animals.

FLIGHT-FROM-HAPPINESS FEAR

This fear prompts action or inaction which will result in termination of contact with, or significantly reduced contact with, a situation, object, or individual(s) which would be of benefit to her. The difference between this fear and the second type is that here the object of fear is something which would increase the quality of health for her—a fact of which the individual is not always aware. In confronting this fear, she quickly withdraws, keeps contact with the source of the fear to a minimum, or ends the situation in which contact is made by creating a diversionary issue.

This reaction is connected with the fear of intimacy, love, vulnerability, success, or being treated with dignity and high regard. They are situations which would be good for her but are also unfamiliar. They are situations which she does not know how to control because of her early life experiences and resulting belief system. She responds by avoiding such situations or by sabotaging them. They are frightening to her because they conflict with her negative beliefs of self, relationships, and the world. It carries the message, "If I am of little worth, then I do not experience healthy people or success-producing situations."

FOR THE VICTIMS

A bright and shiny afternoon.
Schoolyards expelling parcels of energy--
Laughter and play.
To look at these precious beings--
So new, so trusting, so eager--
Makes my heart soar.
To see their smiles
And the sparkle in their eyes--
Brings joy to the hardest heart.

Now look around
and find the child
who drags her feet.
Look into her lifeless eyes.
While most of these young hopefuls
Are going home to love and safety,
This innocent
Is going--
To a nightmare.

SHELLEY

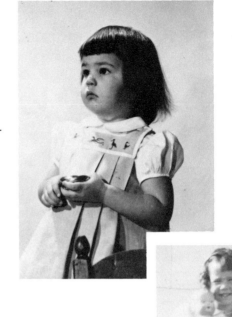

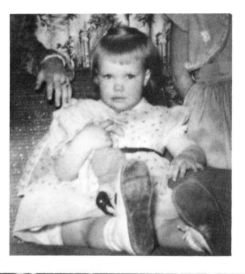

Some examples of flight-from-happiness fear are as follows:

(1) The woman who quickly withdraws from social situations where there are people whom she considers "better than herself," more educated, more religious, or less "damaged."

(2) The woman who finds reason after reason for not going on a date with a man because he is "too nice."

(3) The woman who has great difficulty accepting compliments or celebrations in her honor.

UNDERSTANDING YOUR FEARS

Learn to identify your own fear responses. Keep a journal. Make note of situations you avoid or have difficulty with. Make note of the apparent absence of fears; are you detached from your emotions? Determine if you are moving into self-defeating or self-destructive patterns and should be afraid. Ask yourself some of the following questions:

(1) Do you take unnecessary risks while driving, engaging in hobbies, at work, when traveling, with strangers, etc.?

(2) Do you go for walks at times of the day or at locations that present an unnecessarily high risk for personal injury?

(3) What drugs do you use? How often do you use them? Is it possible you have a substance abuse problem?

(4) Do you find violent men considerably more attractive than men of more controlled or gentle disposition?

(5) Are you most excited by men who are totally controlled, with few emotions and those in positions of power and authority?

(6) Are you excited by bars or other locations which present a high risk of encountering men who are sexually or physically aggressive?

(7) Do you avoid spending time with "normies" -- people who have not been sexually abused?

(8) Do you "not get around to:"
   (a) keeping doctor's appointments,
   (b) registering for school,
   (c) getting your hair done,
   (d) spending time with special friends, or
   (e) asking for help?

(9) Do you experience stress when people try to give you gifts, affection, praise, or love?

(10) Is your attendance at therapy, school, church, weight control programs, or the health spa irregular? Do you begin projects but never quite complete them?

The person who was sexually abused within her family, or was abused outside the family but grew up in a dysfunctional family system, has learned certain fear responses. She has learned the self-preserving fear responses as well as the ones which block her from intimacy, happiness, and success.

Dysfunctional families teach that their perceptions are the only reality, that ideas and experiences outside the family are unacceptable, that challenging the family rules is disloyal, that to belong you must conform to your assigned role in the family, and never do anything to "make the family look bad." A child is taught that all the fears, pains, anger, guilt, and shame of the family are the fears, pains, anger, guilt, and shame of the child. Children are taught to gain reward and acceptance through the same patterns that their parents did.

Pay attention to your emotional health. Notice when you feel and when you do not feel. Lack of feelings can mean something has frightened you and you were not aware of it. Practice being aware of all fear responses and evaluate whether or not they are healthy or unhealthy.

Ask for feedback from a trusted person as to the healthiness of the object of your fear. There are people who are caring and are trustworthy. Do not let one of your health-sabotaging fears keep you from asking for help. By confronting unhealthy fears and diminishing their influences you will increase your personal power and self-esteem. You will be acting on life rather than reacting.

CUES

CUE:
A sensory signal used to identify experiences, facilitate memory, or organize responses. (*The Random House Dictionary of the English Language,* 2nd Ed., 1987)

A "cue" is a sensory experience— sight, sound, smell, taste, or touch—or a combination of experiences in the present which trigger emotional, mental, and/or physical reactions connected to a significant event in the past.

It is not unusual for a victim to doubt her sanity over some confusing and seemingly inexplicable responses she may have observed in herself, responses which seem to be out of her control. These responses are often the result of cues connected to childhood experiences.

A childhood experience which makes a traumatic impression can carry lasting results. A thought or emotion connected to that impressive experience can be activated by a cue. As an adult, the smell of lilacs may bring a sense of happiness or well-being, along with a memory of a childhood spring afternoon when playing with friends or a pet. This same reaction can occur without the exact recall of why the fragrance of the lilacs is so special. In other words, the smell memory activates the feeling without a conscious memory of its origin. This is how cues work, and we are surrounded by them every day.

Present-day reactions to situations or people can be partially or wholly influenced by hidden memories, cues connected to those memories, and the corresponding emotional "charge." All may combine in a person's reaction and action in a given situation without the memory being obvious or the person being conscious of the sensory experience. The cue can facilitate both pleasant experiences and unpleasant experiences.

Clients describe having aversive reactions to individuals or situations which they cannot logically explain. A woman complained that Christmas was such a particularly depressing time of year that she would avoid participating in holiday activities with her husband and children as much as possible. In therapy she remembered that when she was a child, this was the time of year when her stepfather was most sexually and physically abusive. He had "sold her" to some men who had sexually abused her in front of the Christmas tree. The obvious trauma of the incident, combined with the spiritual meaning of the holiday, made that time of year an especially painful one for her.

Another client could not explain why July was such a troublesome and depressing time of year for her. In her recovery process she uncovered a memory of a hot summer evening with her father. The time with him had started very pleasantly with the two of them walking to the store to buy a cold drink. She felt close to him and loved by him. The memory became tragic when she recalled how he changed when they got home, and the night turned into a particularly frightening assault. As an adult, she had difficulty with the peaceful, warm and humid summer evenings just before sunset. She found her anxiety level increasing, and, possessing no apparent explanation, she concluded that there must be something wrong with her. Both of these women uncovered logical explanations for their behaviors and attitudes through therapy programs. They learned to resolve the past, control their emotional reactions, and to participate with friends and family on these special occasions.

A perplexed client once described her discomfort in being around a particular co-worker who was non-threatening in manner and quite likeable as a person. During therapy she was able to identify her problematic reaction as occurring when he leaned over her desk and she smelled his aftershave—the same brand worn by her father when she was a child. Conscious and unconscious memories can hold emotional charges. The time of year, the temperature of the air, a specific animal, and any sensory perception can be a cue connected to the past.

CLAIRE:

I'm angry at my father. I'm scared to death every time people yell. I'm afraid they're going to hurt me because that's what he did to me. I'm afraid of people who drink; I'm afraid of every man I meet who looks like him. I hate Southern Comfort and I can smell it a mile away. I'm afraid of anybody with alcohol on his breath.

Childhood victims are highly sensitized to behaviors and patterns of interactions leading up to abuse. Those sensitivities are carried into adulthood.

This heightened sensitivity combined with childhood traumas means that recovering victims often need to identify numerous cues in their lives. If the smell of a particular drink brought with it a frightening experience on numerous occasions, then the body will automatically anticipate the same event after the original threat is gone. Victims have described an entire range of odors which were at some time cues connected with traumas: dust in an old kitchen cabinet, mothballs in a clothes closet, cigarette smoke, grease and oil in a garage, an orange grove, perspiration, and a hayloft. Clients who quit smoking during their recovery process often report an increased sensitivity to smells and an increased sensitivity to odor cues. This observation leads one to speculate whether one of the original functions of smoking for these victims was to camouflage the disturbing odor.

Tactile experiences can be equally powerful cues. A woman raped as a child by a neighbor carried with her as an adult a strong reaction to body hair. The feel of specific objects, parts of the body, materials, etc., can be cues. Being touched in a specific manner or on specific areas of the body can be cues. A woman who was tied up many times as a child never wore tight bracelets or watches. She also was visibly upset to see others wearing tight objects on their wrists, especially if the objects left marks. She realized she had a problem when her family members pointed out to her that her emotional response was far out of proportion when she and her daughter argued about the daughter's wearing her watch too tightly. The full extent of her childhood abuse had been blocked from memory and was finally finding its way back to her consciousness.

Other victims remembered the feel of freshly pressed cotton, the roughness of a beard or mustache, hard callouses on muscular hands, sharp cinders in an old basement, and the cool softness of damp earth. A woman reported being fearful and having difficulty breathing when her husband would support himself over her during intercourse. In therapy she uncovered a repressed memory. As a small child she was terrified during her abusive experience when the abuser laid his entire weight on her. She believed that she would be smothered and die. The result was that as an adult she had trouble breathing in a similar situation.

MARIE:

For twenty-five years I have had only plastic coat hangers in my home, I would feel uneasy and anxious if I used a wire coat hanger. I never knew why until I remembered that I was sexually abused with a wire hanger. It was only two weeks ago while doing some memory work that I discovered why I've never liked overhead fluorescent lights. . . They remind me of the bright lights used in filming. . .child pornography.

Sights and sounds provide cues also. Victims report anxiety reactions to the sight of a knife, a dark basement, a transient, a straight razor, the male body, wallpaper patterns, a country lane, the color orange, a Christmas ornament, black shoes, a barn, a thick leather belt, and a person of specific body structure or race. They have also described reactions cued by sounds such as a specific song, a leather belt being pulled from its trousers, a tone of voice, specific word phrases or accents, a door being opened, a door being closed or locked, the clinking of whiskey bottles, a beer can being opened, and water running in the shower.

JOYCE:

I remember lying in my bed and hearing my father's footsteps on the stairs, and hearing that belt buckle, and then the door opening and knowing, "Here it comes!" I only recently realized that I flinched each time I heard my husband do the same with his belt when changing out of his work clothes. I never realized why I avoided being around him in the bedroom at that time of day.

Cues are often a combination of many sensory experiences. A client described wanting to bolt from the kitchen one evening as she was preparing to sit down to dinner with her family. She was able to identify several cues of this reaction: the smell of the dish being served, the cacophony of sound created by the voices of her three small children, and her husband's stern voice momentarily put her back in a childhood scenario when her stepfather unexpectedly backhanded her off her chair.

Tastes can be equally potent cues to the past. Persons brutally sexualized may react to the tastes of sperm, urine, sweat, vaginal secretions, etc.. Other tastes may be more indirectly linked to traumas.

JEANIE:

Every Sunday we'd have fried chicken and pretend we were a family. And every Sunday he'd get drunk and late that evening stumble into my bedroom to "say goodnight." To this day, I can't stand fried chicken. It's like it was all part of the ritual. I even have difficulty at family gatherings, like maybe he is going to walk into the house, and he's been dead for two years.

One victim always remembers grape soda because that is what her father used as part of his seduction. Another remembers eggs benedict because that is what her victimizer ordered at nice restaurants when he was in his "good" mood. A specific flavor of ice cream, an alcoholic drink, the salt in perspiration have all been troublesome cues for victims.

Physical ailments or injuries can bring up memories of feelings from the past. A woman who was abused as a child while sick in bed recognized that she felt anxious when she became ill as an adult. Scars resulting from abuse haunt adults. They are painful and persistent daily reminders. A scar from a compound fracture, chronic back pain from having been kicked, cigarette burns, loss of hearing or eyesight, scars on the wrists from attempted suicide, internal injuries—the tragic list goes on and on.

Use a journal to keep a self-inventory. Do you have current emotional reactions which seem irrational or out of proportion to the circumstances? Are there sensory preferences or aversions which you can identify? Pay special attention to those experiences which are most difficult —

illnesses, disagreements, fears, anger, etc. Carefully note all experiences preceding the problematic reaction. Mentally walk through the experience with a trusted friend or therapist. Remember in detail. Ask the person you had a disagreement with to reenact it. It may be that there is no mystery, or it may be a valuable lesson from the past. Pay close attention to what you learn from it.

PHYSICAL BOUNDARIES

BOUNDARY:
Something that indicates or fixes a limit or extent. . . .a separating line. (*Webster's Seventh New Collegiate Dictionary,* 1975)

Everyone needs personal boundaries, both physical and psychological. Each person needs a physical space which she considers hers, a space she prefers that no person enter without her permission. It is a means of privacy. Such is the purpose of locks on a house, a bedroom door, or a bathroom door. Being intruded upon unannounced while in the shower is an invasion of one's physical boundaries. Persons who have been burglarized describe a feeling of having been "violated" or "invaded." They describe this emotional response upon realizing that a total stranger had access to their intimate apparel and belongings.

This sense of "violation" is a small example of what it is like to be sexually abused. Imagine the magnitude of that violation when it is not one's house that is invaded but one's body. This is a violation of the most sacred of boundaries, a boundary every person has a right to have personal control over.

Children are in the early stages of learning about themselves and the world. They integrate experiences into their belief systems with the only logic available—their own inexperienced and naive logic. The beliefs begin to form that "My body is not mine; My body is for people to use; My sexuality is shameful; I am an object for other people's pleasure or abuse." These beliefs are reinforced if the abuse is on more than one occasion. The child may further conclude that "I have no power; I have no control over my life," and specifically, "My body belongs to others." For victims, the concept of boundaries is often confused.

Ask yourself the following questions:

(1) Do people walk in on me in my bedroom or bathroom unannounced, even when the door is closed?

(2) Do the hugs, kisses, touching, or distances some people stand in relationship with me cause me discomfort? Am I unsure how to change that?

(3) Do I often engage in sex even when I do not feel like it?
   (a) Do I do it because it is what my husband wants?
   (b) Do I engage in acts which I do not feel good about?
   (c) Do I do it even when it is painful due to not being lubricated, or for some other reason?

Answering yes to any of the questions above may mean that you need to learn how to set physical boundaries with people. You may need to learn to speak up for yourself and ask for what you need in regard to privacy or personal space. You may need training in parenting and setting limits with children. You may need the help of a therapist in order to feel strong enough and worthy enough to have rights inside and outside your primary relationship. You may need the help of a qualified sex therapist with background understanding of childhood sexual abuse. Your husband or lover may need therapy in order to learn how to be more communicative, more sensitive, or more sharing. Ask for what you need.

FAMILIES

In functional families an individuation process takes place. Family members have separate identities and learn that they have the responsibility for their own individual problems. In functional families, members encourage each other to develop her/his unique talents. The child has much to say in the roles she will play in the family and has the freedom to change roles as she evolves. Feelings and thoughts are acknowledged in the open. In functional families, personalities are distinct, separate and constantly developing in an atmosphere of love and trust.

In dysfunctional families, the family system is more important than the individual. Keeping the patterns of interaction, roles, and beliefs under control is the primary concern. At the center of the dysfunctional family is one person of strongly narcissistic motivation and another person of such insecurity that challenging the rules of the family system is difficult, perhaps inconceivable. The fears, prejudices, angers, and shame of the adults are imposed on the children. There are no individuals, only components of the family. Psychological boundaries do not exist. Weaknesses are not confronted and resolved; they are hidden and protected. The dysfunctions of the adults and family system become the identity of the individuals. The victim cannot see where the problems of others end and her own identity begins. Each person identifies with the dysfunctions. The problems of the family become the child's identity. She cannot imagine life being any other way.

Ask yourself the following questions:

(1) Do I spend more time and energy dealing with my parents than I spend working on the issues within myself or within my primary relationships?

(2) Do I deny what I think or feel around my family of origin so as not to upset them?

(3) Do I often spend time away from my marriage or children to help members of my family of origin with recurring problems of theirs?

Answering yes to any of the above questions may mean that you need to learn to set psychological boundaries with your family of origin. You may still be enmeshed in their system at the expense of your own family or marriage. You may need professional help in breaking free of the dysfunctional bond you still have with these people so that you might be free. You may not know how to encourage these family members to be responsible for themselves. You may need assistance in learning how and when to be responsible for yourself.

Learning to set and maintain healthy boundaries is a vital step in recovery. Assertiveness training is part of the process. Saying no, setting limits, and asking for what is needed are realistic goals. Learn to identify shaming messages and recognize when you are being manipulated. Learn the skills for healthy confrontation.

PSYCHOLOGICAL BOUNDARIES

A recovering victim must learn the skill of separating from others' emotional issues. Compassion and empathy are fine qualities for everyone to practice with moderation and balance. However, the victim too often takes on the pain and suffering of entire groups of people and animals. She has been conditioned to deny her own reality and experience that of others, particularly others in great strife. Part of recovery is learning to let others have their struggles, their pains, and their fears. Rescuing someone else from difficulty or taking away their feelings is denying them a chance to learn. It is denying their experience of reality.

Recovery means learning the process of individuation. This means separating one's own issues from one's parents' issues. It means offering encouragement but letting one's brothers, sisters or parents take responsibility for their own lives. The victim has been taught to jump into a sinking ship and rescue others. She has been taught that no one will swim without her holding them up. The healthiest choice is to lead the way to safety while offering encouragement. Do not to go down with a sinking ship!

A child victim of these circumstances spent so much of her time denying her own reality and adopting her family's reality that she does the same with other groups as an adult. Ask yourself these questions:

(1) When I am around someone at work who is angry or sad, do I come home angry or sad?

(2) Do I sometimes strike out at people my husband is angry with, but whom he will not confront?

(3) Do I dump the anger I feel at work or with my parents on my family, rather than placing it where it belongs?

In a therapy group of women who were victims of child abuse, it is common for camaraderie to develop, a sisterhood. It is a bond of shared experiences. It is a bond of shared triumphs over life-threatening "monsters." Abuse victims report feelings much like those between Vietnam veterans — a closeness, a kinship, and a reluctance to share with "those who have not been there." You can, even in these helpful groups, give away your personal boundaries. You may go home and have nightmares or recurring thoughts about the disturbing events in someone else's childhood. You may "take on" the feelings of someone else. You may walk out of the therapy room and carry home with you the pain of another person's life. Learn to protect yourself.

You may need professional assistance. You may have to sort out whether or not the anxiety you experience is the result of someone else's feelings or a memory being triggered within you. Group will be of little help if each time you go, you take home more problems than those with which you came. Early in therapy, you may need to do nothing other than learn to protect yourself.

BUILDING PROPER PSYCHOLOGICAL BOUNDARIES

Building and maintaining psychological boundaries with people is much more difficult than building physical boundaries. Victims allow other persons' emotions and conflicts to invade or overwhelm them. They have little or no practice in protecting themselves. They have been taught since childhood to embrace others' pains and conflicts. This behavior magnifies their own problems and fulfills their core belief that life is painful or that they are undeserving of contentment.

Victims in recovery have to practice building psychological walls around themselves when in threatening situations. They have to practice internal dialogue of reassurance and protection. They have to be aware of, and screen out, unhealthy or despairing messages in the environment around them. The process is difficult and paradoxical because they must also learn to let the emotional walls down at times of desired intimacy or vulnerability. She must learn to express compassion while simultaneously shielding herself from influences which drag her down or decrease her effectiveness. She must learn to empathize with the struggles of others but not be drawn into depression and take the weight of the world on her shoulders. It is a difficult learning process with many perils. Each person's process and progress is unique because each person's life experiences and resources are uniquely her own. It is a time to be patient and loving with yourself.

IDENTIFYING EMOTIONS

Accurately identifying feelings can be difficult. The physical sensations of joy, fear, pain, and anger are quite similar when measured with scientific instruments. Many women were abused while they were emotionally vulnerable, while experiencing feelings of happiness or joy. For such a victim, accurately identifying her own emotions and then trusting herself in her evaluation is not an easy accomplishment. Add to this the fact that she spent a great amount of her time doubting her own sense of reality due to numerous influences, e.g., defense mechanisms, family dynamics, confused communication patterns, manipulations, and cues. For someone who has believed herself to be shameful all of her life, or struggled to survive for years, or grown up in a family where the daily theme was misery or fear, recognizing and holding onto happiness is a skill that has to be learned and reinforced.

The following excerpt from a women's group therapy session is an example of identifying new feelings:

THERAPIST:
What are you feeling right now?

JEANIE:
I don't know . . . it's weird, kind of twilight zonish.

THERAPIST:

You have just told your father, in the strongest of terms and with what appeared to be great conviction, (using an open chair technique in his absence) that you will no longer keep his secret or carry his shame. How does that feel?

JEANIE:

I don't know that I have ever felt quite like this before. I'm not sure what it is.

THERAPIST:

Well, do you feel weak or strong?

JEANIE:

Strong. In fact, I feel larger physically, taller maybe. Does that make sense? (checking out reality with others)

THERAPIST:

You are sitting taller now than you were thirty minutes ago.

JEANIE:

Really?

THERAPIST:

Ask your friends what they see.

GROUP MEMBERS:

The other women comment on the increased color in her face, relaxed manner, and general softness.

JEANIE:

(tears)

THERAPIST:

What are the tears about?

JEANIE:
I love them all so much. (the group members)

THERAPIST:
Anything else?

JEANIE:
I love that child who got used.

THERAPIST:
So what are you feeling?

JEANIE:
I don't know.

THERAPIST:
Is it joy?

JEANIE:
Oh, God yes! (more tears) I always thought it was my fault!.

THERAPIST:
Would you be willing to share your happiness with your friends and help make it real for yourself?

JEANIE:
Yes! (hugging and tears from other members)

THERAPIST:
Are you still feeling it? (her answer of yes) Be that taller person, let the feeling grow, and tell everyone what it is like. Also tell them how hard you have worked to get to this moment.

JEANIE (later explaining):
I have always known in my head that it wasn't my fault. I mean a seven-year-old didn't cause it. But for the first time in my life, I

actually felt free of the "monster." When that happened, I was
overwhelmed with tears of happiness.

HEALTHY EMOTIONAL AWARENESS

People who grew up in dysfunctional families have little experience with healthy emotional awareness. They know how to be sensitive to danger, fears of all kinds, and shame. They are practiced at feeling for others — abused children, starving people, and homeless pets, to name a few. But to spontaneously experience and express the entire range of emotions from extreme sadness to unbridled joy is a new phenomenon. Years of coping, defending, or mistrusting have taught repression, not expression.

A lifetime of distorted, manipulative, and dishonest communications leaves an adult confused about many emotions and their meanings. She may experience and internally react to situations, then attribute her reaction to a false cause. Habitual defenses, cues, unhealthy fears, shame, or dysfunctional beliefs keep her from understanding the nature and origin of her feelings.

AFFIRMING YOUR FEELINGS

The process of being sensitive to, identifying, holding onto, and celebrating the internal state called happiness is not an easy task for someone who has been taught she is undeserving of such an experience and that she cannot trust such an unfamiliar feeling. It is like being given a piece of delicious candy after having had candy consistently stolen away all of her life. It is difficult to trust others, and it is difficult to trust herself or her own perceptions. As a child she had drawn the conclusion that it was easier to never get up rather than to get knocked down again.

Messages from the abuser or family of origin influence current efforts to interpret life and identify feelings. The abuser may have told the child that what he was doing was loving her. She had no other experiences from which to measure the accuracy of this information. It was provided by a trusted adult "who knows better than children." She may have been taught to deny or doubt her own experience of feelings like sadness or anger with statements like, "Stop your crying or I'll give your something to cry about;" "Don't you raise your voice to me;" and "Your puppy has gone to heaven. Now don't be sad, we will get you another."

Even in the healthiest families, affirming a child's feelings is often overlooked or discouraged. It is most often neglected by adults who are not comfortable with their own emotions or confused by what they feel. In seriously dysfunctional families, the existence of emotions, the identification of emotions, and the expression or honoring of emotions is lacking. The victim ends up guessing what her emotional reality is. She ends up looking to others to tell her what she ought to feel, and thereby denies her own internal reality.

LORRI:

I can remember my mother saying things like, "But we're a family;" "He's your father and loves you;" or "So many other kids have it worse than you." So I'd feel ashamed for wanting out and crazy because somewhere in the back of my head was a voice saying, "There's got to be more to life than this!"

Victims are survivors. The strength it takes to survive is the same strength it takes to gain and keep the experiences of joy and happiness as her real self is set free. For a victim, joy and happiness need not be fleeting moments between trials of pain and fear. If you are experiencing joy in a roomfull of angry or fearful people, fight to hang onto it. Let them have their trials, but you hang onto your feelings! Many victims describe their anger that the so-called "average" people of the world do not recognize the realities of abuse in the world. This position is well taken! It is also true that joy and happiness in life are real. Believe in the positive realities as well as the negative ones. Confront the influences in your environment which tempt you to give your reality away, and confront the influences within yourself which trick you into doing the same. Work everyday to change dysfunctional core beliefs, the disturbing cues, and habitualized defenses that no longer serve any useful purpose. Practice letting peace and joy occupy a regular part of your new core belief system.

ANDREA'S STORY

What is it like to be controlled from a child's perspective? What is it like to have one's personal boundaries invaded when you are only nine years old? Andrea was a client of ours. Her description of her abuse is presented exactly as she wrote it for us. Punctuation and a few words have been inserted by the authors for clarity. It was too painful for Andrea to write the story in the first person, so she wrote a story about a "little girl" — her little girl.

ANDREA:

There once lived a family who had a mom, a stepdad, sometimes an older daughter and a younger daughter. When the grandmother died they moved in with (the) grandfather. When they lived with the grandfather he became kind of like a father to the younger daughter because the stepdad was gone a lot, as he was in the navy. He never really acted as if he liked the younger daughter during the day. He liked her at night. When he was home he'd come in at night before she went to bed and touch her breasts and stick his hand down her P.J.'s. He always told her it was O.K. Before he left her though he'd tell her not to tell her mother. Or she'd be bad.

Then the little girl grew up and her dad came home from being overseas. She missed her (step)dad because her grand-dad died and she was very lonely. He left her like her stepdad and grandmother did. She was sad. She was glad when her stepdad came home because she thought her family would be happy again. She hated being an only child most of the times. When her (step)dad came home he argued more and more about her to her mother telling her mother she was no good and a tramp, but then at night she'd wake up and her dad would be happy with her again. He'd be good to her. She didn't feel so lonely, or bad.

The girl took naps on a big green couch. Her dad would wake her up and then he'd tell her that it was time that she learned about life and he'd pin her down on the couch and get on top of her and force (her) to kiss him. Then he'd unbutton her blouse and feel her

breasts; then he'd unbutton her pants and take them off of her.
He'd put that thing in her and keep her pinned down. No matter
how hard she tried to get away he'd hold her so she couldn't.
When he'd finish she'd cry and he would slap her and hit her with
his belt and tell her to stop crying and if she told her mom he'd kill
her.

One day though he couldn't stop her from crying. Her bird died
and he blamed her for it and chased her into her mom's room. He
hit her in the face and on the stomach with his belt. She kicked him
with shoes on and got away and locked herself in the bathroom. He
tried to break the door down, but he couldn't, and then her mom
came home. She asked him what (was) happening. He said
nothing. Then she asked her daughter and she couldn't hold back
any more and so she told her. The mom went outside and talked
(to) the stepdad. He tried to deny it but didn't. She told him to get
out. He said it was her daughter's word against his, and that maybe
he'd just kill them all. He left finally, but the girl hated her house
and the green couch. They scared her and she was afraid to look at
them or be near them. So she'd stay out a lot. She hated where she
lived and everybody around her.

The physical and sexual abuse that Andrea experienced are
obvious. The psychological abuse is more subtle. Andrea was starved for
affection and attention. This need was exploited by her victimizer. She was
a victim of control; control through intimidation and control through the
exploitation of the natural desires of an emotionally neglected child. Her
sense of reality was distorted; her sense of self beaten down.

Fortunately Andrea's mother found help for both herself and
Andrea, and Andrea now has a chance to have what is every child's birthright: the right to be nourished and protected and loved, the right to unfold
and develop and know herself as her Creator intended her to be.

POWER

Imagine power as a mighty, thoroughbred racehorse and yourself as the rider. A responsible person rides with direction and purpose. There are others who ride recklessly, without regard for the welfare of themselves or others. They trample over anyone in their path and gallop off in one direction or another without thought of the consequences. Responsible power is focused. Decisions and plans in life are carefully chosen and implemented. Small goals are set and worked toward. Small victories lead to the setting and achieving of larger goals. All riders, even expert equestrians, are thrown occasionally. Few experiences in life are without setbacks and detours. Belief in oneself encourages a rider to "re-mount" and try again.

Power is a phenomenon with many dimensions and types of expression. Power is the awareness of the availability of options and the freedom to choose any of those options. Responsible power includes commitment to growth, confronting fears, and taking responsibility for one's own life. It is making choices with consideration for both one's own welfare and that of others. A woman who uses power appropriately inspires rather than coerces; she is a catalyst rather than a manipulator; she offers encouragement and support rather than threats or intimidation.

The human need for predictability can set a person up for serious self-deception. When a child is born, she has a road map of life before her with infinite possible courses. There will be roads which travel through territory with people of compassion and love, and others through territory filled with persons who are manipulative, abusive and exploitive. There will be experiences of exhilarating adventure, hard work, great rewards, and bitter disappointments. Great is the potential of the child who receives loving guidance on her journey.

For the child who endures abuse and receives little or no assistance, the possibilities and potential diminish. What if she is shamed and represses the memories of pain? What if she is taught that she is unlovable? How is she going to meet and feel comfortable with people who will treat her like she is a valuable human being when she has been taught that she is of little value? People who are shaming and abusive are familiar persons in her life. People who do not use shame or abuse others are unfamiliar to the child who grew up neglected or abused. If she was not taught that she deserved to be treated well as a child, she will not believe that she is worthy of nourishing relationships as an adult.

The adult abused as a child gained what little control she could by manipulating and defending. As a child, it was what she had to do to survive. Her control is that of a reactor, not an initiator. Her personal power is weakened by doubts about self-esteem and fears of being "found out" in relationships. How can she establish predictability and control? How can she realize and expand her personal power? She can begin by identifying the faulty beliefs she developed as a child. She can proceed with the emotional work of letting go of these dysfunctional beliefs and replacing them with healthy ones. She can identify the ways in which she learned to control herself, relationships, and other areas of her life. What are the fears, cues, life beliefs and experiences that limited her? The more awareness, education, and implementation of new patterns in which she engages, the more freedom she will enjoy. Power is the freedom to choose.

THE APPROPRIATE USE OF POWER

As a woman uses power appropriately she experiences an increasing sense of serenity and balance in her life. She gives to others but is not emptied by the giving. She takes from others but does not empty them. She recognizes that she is responsible for herself. She wants the best for others but does not take away their responsibility for achieving it. She provides support but clearly recognizes the need of each individual to develop her own resources. She respects and facilitates others in their own journeys of self discovery.

A woman who uses power judiciously allows herself to feel joy and sorrow with equal vigor. She expresses righteous anger but is not vindictive. She works toward resolutions in which everyone is a winner. She is motivated by self-expression and creativity rather than competition and greed.

Responsible use of power includes confronting injustices in ways which enhance one's own dignity and that of the person or persons being confronted. A responsible and powerful woman listens for the truth in criticisms leveled at her with genuine concern and love, but she does not give up her self-worth in the process. She protects herself from those who criticize in an attempt to shame her and make her less of a person. She is willing to acknowledge her mistakes and makes amends when possible. She recognizes her own fears and faces them with confidence and courage. She regularly commits herself to life with a courage she is not always sure she has.

Understand that what you believe of yourself, the life circumstances which are most familiar and predictable to you, and the behavior patterns in which you engage, have all been learned. You have the power to change your belief system. You can learn to believe differently of yourself. You can learn how to establish a healthy environment, both physically and psychologically. You can learn functional strategies for controlling aspects of your life which are within your control. You can learn to accept aspects of your life that are not within your control. As you learn and grow, you are no longer just surviving; you are unfolding. You are no longer just coping; you are empowered.

Native Americans hold a belief that the most powerful of the four basic elements — fire, air, earth and water — is water. Everflowing around much harder substances, ultimately wearing the jagged granite smooth, it flows inexorably toward its destination. Like water in the stream of life, a powerful woman may be diverted around obstacles and run up against jagged edges, but she continues toward her destination.

6

RELATIONSHIPS AND SEXUALITY

I don't know what love is. I've never experienced it. I don't know what this thing is that other people talk about, people who get married, and are at peace with themselves, and live in little white houses, with two children and all the stuff in the movies and the books. I've read all about it. I know all about it, but I've never felt it. *MARIE*

INTRODUCTION

Most of the women who pick up this book will have identified themselves as "the problem" in their intimate personal relationships. After all, "I was the victim, and I am the one with all these complications in life, right?"

It is true that the victim's troubles may be what is called in counseling, the "presenting problems." But do not jump to the conclusion that you are the "sick" one or the only one with issues to confront. You may have hidden parts of yourself, held back, or avoided feelings, thoughts, or behaviors. You may have behaved in ways that caused pain and difficulties for yourself and for others.

Believe us when we tell you that there have been some payoffs in this behavior for your partner, some advantages in these "rules of the game." Perhaps your partner has as many frailties as you. Perhaps the limited intimacy has fit your partner's insecurities as well as yours. Perhaps your partner is used to the predictability of your relationship, no matter how dysfunctional it has become.

RELATIONSHIP CHALLENGES

If you decide to grow, then your partner will be challenged to grow also. If you begin to feel differently and act differently, if you intend to have more and give more in life, then your partner will be facing major life changes of his own. All change, even obviously positive change, is frightening.

It is vitally important for you to recognize that your partner has his own issues to face. Labeling one or the other of you as "the patient" may serve to begin the therapeutic process, but labeling one of you as the "sick one" serves little purpose other than to reassure the fragile ego of the "non-sick" person.

In a partnership there are shared life issues to be confronted and each partner has a responsibility to face his or her portion. Each person has a responsibility to identify and face the issues that are uniquely one's own. If you have acquiesced all of your life to male authority figures, then you have a personal responsibility to learn new patterns of assertiveness and self-expression. If your partner has assumed a dominant authority role all of his life, he has a personal responsibility to learn new patterns of cooperation and encouragement in the creation of an equal partnership. Both of you have a responsibility to grieve the loss of old and familiar roles that are no longer appropriate. Both of you need to make a commitment to yourselves and to each other to giving up those roles in favor of new and healthier ones.

Many of the women reading this book will be in what they believed at one time was a healthy love relationship. You may discover during your therapy and growth that your partner is quite comfortable with things the way they are. You may also discover that your partner sometimes sabotages your attempts to break free of negative beliefs of self, dysfunctional behavior patterns, and lack of assertiveness. Some of you will detect this resistance to change in friends, family, and even some professionals. To continue to grow, you will need to make some difficult and painful choices.

At times you will have to take a stand and have the courage to defend it. You will need to use righteous anger to defend yourself and demand that an issue be faced or a behavior changed. For many of you this will be your first significant act of self-love. It may be the first time as a former victim that you assert and maintain your perception of reality and commitment to health as an individual and in a relationship. The relationship will grow in trust and intimacy as issues are worked through. If you are not heard, if you are ignored or abused, if the working through is consistently sabotaged, then the relationship will stagnate or fail.

You may discover that there are people in your life that choose not to resolve issues with you. This may be due to the other person's fears, ignorance, or lack of courage. It is up to you to decide if the relationship is worth "putting on hold" or if you need to let go of it.

This is a tough decision, a decision that no one can make for you. It is personal and lonely. Ignoring it or letting it remain unresolved is one choice that you have. Rationalizing or isolating is also a choice. It is your timetable and your life. Be aware that to choose to grow, to break free of the past traumas, to be the person you are capable of being requires the determination and willingness to make decisions and the courage to take responsibility for those decisions.

TAKING CARE OF YOU

There are readers of this book who have never experienced a truly loving and committed relationship. You may believe that such a thing is impractical or occurs only in romance novels. You may reject the concepts or even ridicule them. This is understandable. You have been hurt deeply in your life and trust is not easily given. You have needed to take care of yourself because nobody else would. You may be alone in your life or in a destructive relationship. Some of you may even fear for your life in the relationship in which you are currently involved.

Take care of your physical and emotional safety. This may mean sharing this book only with persons that you trust. It may mean playing one role during part of the day, in order to survive or build courage, and nurturing new thoughts and feelings at private moments. Seek knowledge and help where and when you can. Protect your children as you need to and give them help and knowledge when you can. If you are alone or afraid, begin your recovery by becoming connected with other persons that you trust.

We cannot emphasize enough the importance of a strong support system. Remember that it took you many years to learn the behaviors and attitudes that you now practice. Be gentle with yourself and give yourself time to learn and trust new behaviors and attitudes. Take small risks and set achievable goals for being free to love and be loved. Remember above all that you are not alone, defective or shameful. You can love yourself and experience intimacy with a partner. Others have done it before you. Others are doing it at this moment. They are there to show you the way. You can make the choice to reach out, to help yourself and to allow others to support you in a recovery program.

ROMANCE AND RELATIONSHIPS

It is in our intimate personal relationships that strengths and weaknesses of character most quickly surface. When we spend long periods of time with another person, it is almost impossible not to reveal conscious and subconscious fears and shortcomings through actions, confrontations, subjects talked about, and subjects avoided. Maturity occurs when people confront one another within the context of significant relationships.

It is a common misconception that a healthy love relationship is one in which the initial romantic euphoria remains constant throughout the duration of the relationship. People describe this experience in a variety of ways: fireworks, excitement, lust, turn-on, rush, thrill, mystery. Couples often go through a variety of behaviors in an attempt to sustain this euphoria when it begins to decrease in intensity. In actuality, persons in a healthy, maturing relationship will outgrow the initial, intensely romantic, and idealized perceptions. The couple will reach a point in their relationship when the realities and responsibilities become more apparent. Each can recognize and acknowledge that his/her partner is not the answer to all his/her insecurities and problems.

When the initial romance of a relationship abates, each of us still has to deal with the emotional and psychological issues that we have carried within us all along. These issues have not been miraculously banished by the romance; they are on hold temporarily. At the same time that we need to acknowledge the realities of the relationship, our partner is revealing his own issues after having suppressed them throughout the courtship stage.

Contrary to popular belief (and yearning), love does not conquer all; that is, not love in the sense of romance or feelings. It is not easy to acknowledge that a significant part of what we believed to be admirable attributes in our primary partner was embellished by us in the initial romantic glow. Objectivity has a way of cooling the most ardent of flames.

By now you may be thinking that we are overly pessimistic and cynical about romance. Not so! What we have to share is actually very good news for persons interested in "growing up." It is at this critical point of honest evaluation that a relationship can evolve into something truly mature and loving. It is an opportune time for each partner to confront the issues of the past, which can haunt a person until they are resolved. When two persons are committed to a common goal of maturity they will experience both fear and joy. It is a time for fearing the unknown in the future and the changes required within each of us. It is a time of joy because we realize that so much is possible.

THE STRENGTH OF A COMMITTED RELATIONSHIP

When there is a firm, mature commitment between two persons, fear and joy can be shared openly. When there is commitment, each partner trusts the other to see issues through to resolution, to a growing level of maturity and understanding. With each issue resolved comes an increased sense of freedom, personal power, and joy.

Loving confrontation is an inherent part of any committed relationship. There is a commitment to enjoying life together and a commitment to growth. Each partner is invested in the health of the other. One partner will not stand idly by as the other self-destructs or harms others. Each partner is invested in helping the other realize all the strengths he/she has as an individual and as a couple. Each is committed to becoming the best possible individual she/he can be. Each is committed to the relationship. The result of each personality unfolding, and the relationship becoming the best it can be, results in synergism, that mysterious phenomenon when one plus one equals three. The payoffs of the relationship are greater than the sum of its parts. Both partners benefit to a degree they had not previously known existed. Happiness, joy, and serenity are the by-products of a committed relationship built on loving confrontation and maturity.

Many people make the mistake of believing that a committed relationship is a "safe-house" from a hostile world. In a sense, home is a refuge. It is a place of love, unconditional acceptance, and safety. But it is not a place from which to escape the responsibilities of life and one's own maturation process. A healthy and vital relationship is not a place for hiding from the situations in life which will challenge a person to grow. In a healthy, committed relationship, each partner is supportive, sensitive, and loving, while also being honest, responsible, and confrontive. It is vital to each person's maturity to not be "taken care of," "covered for," or encouraged in unhealthy dependency. There are times in a growing relationship when one partner says to the other, "There are some issues here that you and I must face." Both partners are committed to resolution of the issues blocking the growth of closeness, trust, and appreciation of life. Both people are committed to the growth of intimacy.

It is our wish that every woman reading this book will have in her life someone who is loving, supportive, and committed to the betterment of their relationship. It is also our hope that as a couple they will engage in loving confrontation. It is further our wish that every family member of a victim learn how to lovingly confront the victim and be open themselves to being confronted.

SEXUALITY AND CUES

LORRI:
It feels like a monster—allowing myself to have sexual feelings.
If I did and got involved then I'd feel dirty all over again. I
never have talked about this before, but it's true. Sex and talk
about sex and sexual feelings scare me. As long as there's no
chance of a real sexual involvement, I'm OK. The minute sex
might really happen, I run like hell in the opposite direction.
It scares me; it brings up too much pain.

In Chapter Five we explained that sensory experiences can elicit emotional, mental and behavioral reactions rooted in a victim's childhood. For a victim of sexual abuse, these cues will manifest themselves most ramatically in sexual relationships. Thoughts of sex, anticipation of sexual

timacy, or any sensory component of a sexual interaction can cue an

notional or physical reaction that originated in the past. Smells, touches, sounds, tastes, or sights with any connotation of sexuality can trigger the same emotional reaction a woman experienced in her abuse as a child.

MARIE:

Within seconds or minutes of feeling good about sex, I'm hit with a tidal wave of shame and guilt.

BECKY:

When I feel sexual, I feel shameful. . . I always have, for as long as I can remember, felt that I am a bad person. . . that sex is bad and that I deserve to be hurt.

Most persons, whether overtly abused or not, experience some shame about their sexuality. It is a part of socialization in our culture. For the child victim of sexual abuse the message of shame is particularly power-ful. It can make adult sexual experiences seem frightening and painful, and create despair and conflict within its victim.

Mental images can be the result of cues or they can be the cues themselves. Clients describe experiencing flashbacks or "blips," brief images in which they envision a past abusive experience. They are not always sure if the experience is a memory or not, but report experiencing strong emotional reactions concurrent with the flashback. These flashbacks can occur during sleep, causing disturbances and dreams which then influence the emotional state in which a person awakens. The process can also work in reverse. Sensory experiences can trigger images, flashbacks, or sleep disturbances.

Within the context of sexuality, a special type of cue response is common in abuse victims. It is a sensory experience which triggers an unconscious defense mechanism. Any part of a sexual encounter can cue habitualized defenses — a specific word, an odor, a manner of touching. A victim will describe "going dead," "leaving," or "turning off" when these cues are triggered.

CLAIRE:

As soon as a man touches me I just go "dead" and block everything off. And I don't even know if I want to or not. It feels like I can't move. So I just stay away from all men. I protect myself by not letting anyone get close to me.

Claire describes how swiftly old coping mechanisms are activated in situations similar to those in which she experienced abuse as a child. She describes her response as being outside her conscious choosing. Cues can elicit a response with such power and swiftness that the woman is convinced that she is powerless to control her response. As a little girl Claire dissociated or isolated to cope with the stress of her abuse. Her mind implemented a psychological process to protect itself. For Claire the process became habituated and is activated in any situation of a similar nature, such as the possibility of sexual intimacy with a partner.

LANA:

Having intercourse is not the problem. The problem is intimacy -- being vulnerable with someone means risking getting hurt again.

An habitualized defense mechanism such as "isolation" is cued by a sensory experience during a sexual encounter. This phenomenon is logical when viewed in the context of its origin. When the child first used it, it was to protect herself from a hostile environment. It was a useful tool that may have saved her sanity and her life. It becomes a handicap in adulthood when the original threat is no longer present and the woman is striving for vulnerable and loving expressions with her partner. Victims' descriptions of this phenomenon are consistent: "I blank out," "my thoughts get all scrambled," "I just shut down," and "I'm not there anymore."

MICHELLE:

When I think someone is trying to "corner" me and get sexual, I become really confused and afraid. Sometimes I don't even know where I am.

Michelle's reaction is a common one among victims of abuse. One of the ways she coped in childhood with violence and psychological abuse was to dissociate; she would "blank out." By repeatedly focusing her thoughts away from what was happening to her, she did not have to be fully conscious of the abuse as it was occurring. As an adult, Michelle experiences "automatic" confusion whenever she perceives the possibility of pain or fear in a sexual relationship. She is utilizing her original coping mode.

TO BE FEMALE

Many of the dimensions inherent to being female act as cues to strong physical reactions, emotions, memories and defense mechanisms. Our culture's attitudes towards the uniquely female experience of menarche accounts for some of these problems. For women who grew up in seriously dysfunctional families, the onset of the menstrual cycle brings added stresses. If a young girl is repeatedly shamed as she experiences this natural biological function, she will experience feelings of shame about her sexuality as an adult. Abuses in childhood about what it means to be female are numerous — crude jokes about femininity, obscene language, incorrect information or no information at all. Many clients have described the terror they felt when they began their first menstrual cycle and feared that they were bleeding to death. For others, the onset of menses was considered of so little importance that they had to improvise materials to use as tampons. Any of these abusive experiences can cause continued stress during a woman's menstrual cycle, causing not only psychological, but physical stress as well. Irregularity and interruption of menses are not uncommon. What role childhood sexual abuse may play in pre-menstrual syndrome (PMS) has not been adequately researched or established. What is true of the women that we have seen is that a high percentage of them suffer from this problem.

Visits to a doctor or hospital can cue responses connected to past abuse. Doctors are usually male and represent strong authority figures. The female patient is in a subordinate position. The doctor is in control of the situation and any interactions. The patient is asked to trust and follow instructions. She experiences the relationship as one in which she is asked to be vulnerable and submissive, much the same role she played as a child victim. Breast exams, pap smears, and various gynecological procedures can be stressful, even terrifying, for someone victimized as a child. Medical procedures often include being physically probed and prodded, regarded as an object, and having objects inserted into one's body. These procedures are often similar in nature to the childhood abuse. Doctors need to be educated to the sensitivity needed by their patients.

MARIE:
As a child I learned that if I did not say that my broken bones, concussions and abrasions were from "accidents," that I would be even more battered. I was forty years old before I told a doctor that the scar on my arm was from my father breaking it.

Often there are old injuries and scars which are a result of your childhood abuse. Acknowledging this reality can bring up old feelings of shame and the responsibility not to tell "the secret." If medical attention is a problem for you, seek out doctors with whom you feel comfortable and who will listen to your needs and opinions. Trust your instincts and do not allow yourself to be further victimized by thoughtless or unfeeling persons. You deserve to be treated with respect and consideration. Remember that loving yourself includes taking care of both body and mind. Treat yourself well, even if you do not yet feel you deserve it. Trust that if you treat yourself well, the "deserving" feeling will follow.

JEANIE:
I protect myself from men just like I protected myself from my stepfather. I hide the "real" me. I always hold something back.

LORRI:
In my entire life, I've never been intimate with anyone.

The recovering victim may not always be aware that she is defending herself from her feelings. As a child the defense mechanisms became habituated and she may not have had any adult experiences of being sexual without them. It has been "reality" for as long as she can remember. She cannot recall a time when she believed any differently. Regardless of her perceptions, there was a time when she was not afraid or ashamed of her sexuality. There was a time when she did not need to defend herself. This time was before the abuse and the resultant shame. Children are not born feeling shameful, angry, sad, or fearful of their sexuality. These reactions are learned; they are the result of experience. If a child's early experiences with sexuality involve stress and trauma, then psychological defending is necessary. The habituated use of defense mechanisms distorts reality by numbing the user emotionally and psychologically. Both partners must be emotionally and mentally present to fully appreciate a loving sexual experience.

SEXUAL COMPULSIVITY

SHEILA:
My husband and I acted out things that included pornography; we talked about our past sexual experiences, we talked about making it with other people. We talked about sexual things all the time for about a year, and then we began to really do some of them.

We have already observed that some former childhood victims have no trouble being orgasmic or pleasing their partners. If this sexual lifestyle creates no problems and is fulfilling, then they have one less issue to confront in their growth process. There is, however, a group of recovering victims that struggle with being excessively preoccupied and controlled by their own sexuality. For these women, sex is compulsive. It is a means of sabotaging intimacy, denying feelings and avoiding any psychological work that needs to be done before a person can experience sexual intimacy.

Most women who were victimized as children were abused by someone who was sexually compulsive. It was by someone who became pre-occupied, set up a ritualization and acted on it. Some former victims will find themselves attracted to the same personality types in intimate relationships as adults. You may find that you are playing the complementary role, or co-addict role, to someone with serious sexually addictive patterns.

ILLUSTRATION 6A

THE ADDICTION CYCLE

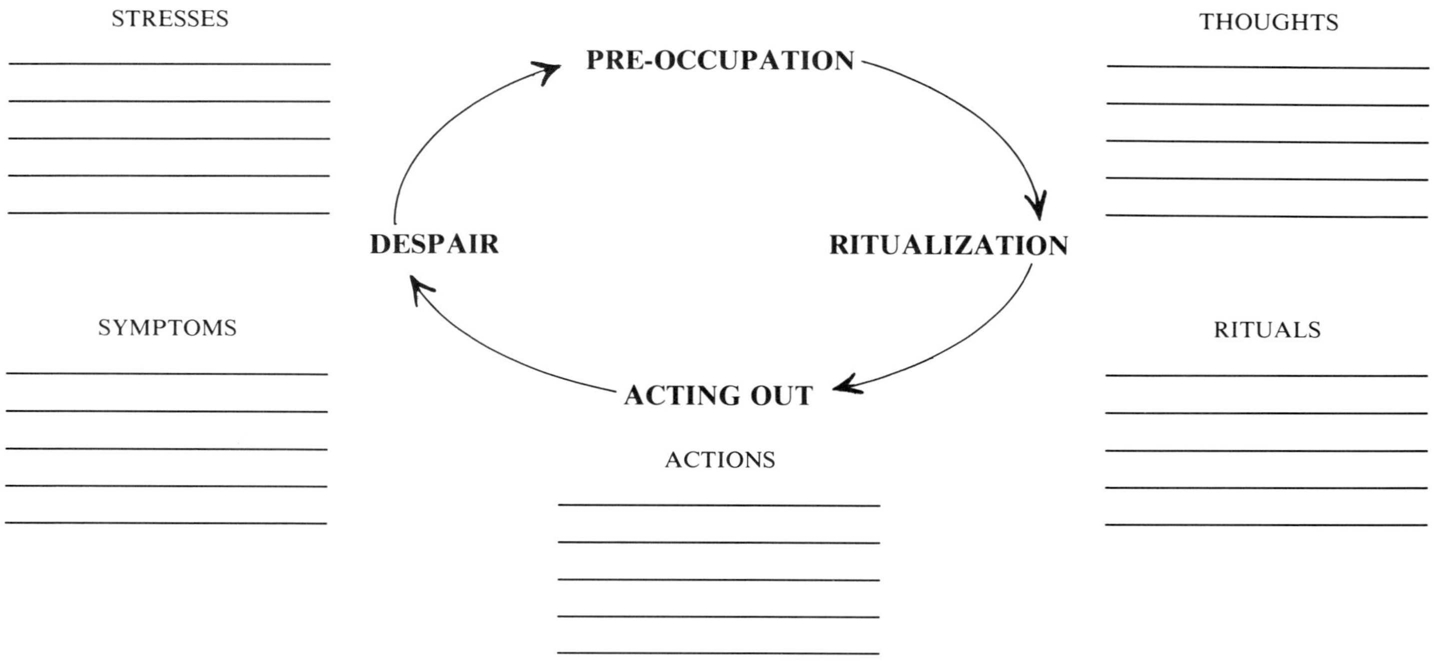

STRESSES

SYMPTOMS

DESPAIR

PRE-OCCUPATION

ACTING OUT

RITUALIZATION

ACTIONS

THOUGHTS

RITUALS

CHART YOUR ADDICTION CYCLE

Identify: 1) the *stresses* that precipitate the cycle; 2) the *thoughts* you have when you preoccupy; 3) the *rituals* you go through as you prepare to act out; 4) your specific behavior (*actions*) when you act out; and 5) the *symptoms* you experience in despair.

For an expert delineation of sexual addiction and co-addiction, we recommend Dr. Patrick Carnes' pioneering work in the field of compulsive sexual behavior. Patrick Carnes, Ph.D., has devoted his book, *Out Of The Shadows, Understanding Sexual Addiction,* to the examination and treatment of this behavior pattern. Carnes says sex can be an addiction just as much as alcohol or drugs. For many persons with compulsive personalities, sexual thoughts or sexual behaviors become self-destructive and damaging to relationships. In our clinical practice we have successfully treated compulsive sexual behavior using an addiction model.

To determine whether or not you are caught in a compulsive behavior pattern, educate yourself about the subjects of sexual addiction and co-dependency. Make a searching and honest inventory of your life. Ask for and listen to honest feedback from family, friends and colleagues that you trust. Consult with a professional who has expertise in treating compulsive behaviors. Persons caught up in compulsions and addictions are masters of rationalization. Denial and delusion enable them to talk themselves out of seriously confronting difficult issues, confrontations which could dramatically improve the quality of their lives.

UNDERSTANDING THE ADDICTION CYCLE

An addiction cycle consists of four identifiable stages. (See Illustration 6A.) The stages are often not clearly distinguishable but will overlap. The stages may require days or weeks to proceed through— or a complete cycle may take place in minutes or hours. Each addict's cycle is unique to her specific situation. For the person caught in a sexually addictive cycle, sexual thoughts or behaviors become a "fix," a way to avoid resolving problems, a tool for sabotaging intimacy, and a means of achieving isolation. For a sex addict, sex can be a high which provides an escape into momentary excitement. The excitement is temporary and followed by depression or despair.

DENISE:
When I was a kid I thought that if I was sexual with a person who was smart, I would get smart. If I was sexual with a person with

*good qualities, I would have them too. I spent long hours thinking
about sex, thinking and watching for partners to make me be a
better person.*

Sexual addiction is a learned pattern of behavior, the result of
being taught at an early age that self-worth is to be found in sexuality. If a
primary caretaker in a person's childhood reinforces sexually provocative
behavior with attention or affection, then it logically follows that as an adult
one will seek affirmation in the same manner.

MARIE:
*I was looking for a person to fill the empty spaces with love. But it
never happened. It was just fucking. I was looking and looking
and acting out (being sexual) trying to find somebody to love me. I
had this conviction, this core belief, that nobody was ever going to
really love me.*

For a woman caught in an addictive behavior pattern, stress is
often a precipitating factor. She struggles with moments of fear, pain,
anger, shame, or despair. These may be cued by real or imagined threats.
They may be the result of current problems or the result of memories from
the past. They may be the result of events outside her control, or they may
be the direct result of her own actions or inactions. Once a person is in
the grips of an addictive behavior pattern she unconsciously "sets herself
up" for situations in which she can act out sexually and then rationalize
her behavior.

RHONDA:
*A lot of my preoccupation is about how afraid I am of losing my
partner. I decide that I'm the only one who cares about the relationship, the only one working on it. I'm so afraid of the hassle if
I confront him (the partner). It's easier to get a new partner.*

ANNETTE:

After awhile I start thinking that I'm not important (in the relationship). I just don't feel needed by my partner anymore. My delusion is that sex means a good relationship, that sex will make me feel wanted, loved, needed.

PREOCCUPATION

In the "preoccupation" stage of an addiction cycle, an addict begins to obsess about sexuality and being sexual. The thoughts generate feelings of excitement or pleasure, diminishing the pain of anxieties that the addict is experiencing in other areas of her life. An addict may fantasize about people other than her primary partner, about sexual acts which violate her value system, and about self-destructive scenarios. Her thoughts may bring fear, shame, excitement, or a combination of these emotions. The thoughts are compulsive and persistent and she begins to obsess about acting out.

JACKIE:

I would visualize the whole thing in my mind. I would consider such things as the time, the place, what I would wear, what we would talk about. It was like writing a play and then acting it out.

RHONDA:

Anger is a part of my ritualization. As soon as I get angry with my present partner, I give myself permission to start fantasizing. I run out of the house and drink or do drugs. I go out and "cruise," looking for someone to "love" me.

RITUALIZATION

The "preoccupation" stage is followed by the "ritualization" stage, the stage in which an addict begins to actively or passively arrange for an opportunity to act out sexually. Each addict has her own "M.O." (*modus operandi*, or method), her own particular ritual that she follows. If an addict compulsively engages in extramarital affairs, she may begin flirting with a co-worker. This may be followed by lunch or drinks together. Her excitement builds as she anticipates the next step. She may fantasize about being discovered or what the new sexual experience will be like. Ritualization is a scenario or progression of events leading up to acting out sexually.

DENISE:

I found that during the acting out my breathing and heart rate would go way up. The pounding of my heart was so loud to me that I was sure others must be able to hear it, too. I felt like I was going to explode. It was a tremendous, single-minded intensity. The risk involved just added to the excitement. In those moments, I felt like no one or no thing in the world could stop me.

ACTING OUT

In the "acting out" stage the addict is totally in the grip of her addiction, and unable to stop her compulsive behavior. The need for a "fix" or a "high" is so intense that she loses all caution and will allow nothing to stand in her way. With reckless disregard for her own safety and that of others, she is a runaway train on a track to destruction. In the early stages of sexual compulsivity, simply flirting with possible sexual scenarios may be the acting out stage. As a sex addict continues repeating the addiction cycle, however, she will need more and more of her "drug of choice" — sexual acting out. She will seek out more dangerous or forbidden behavior to achieve the requisite "fix."

SHEILA:

I feel so rotten the next day. I apologize for being such a rotten wife. I tell my husband that it will never happen again, and we kiss and make up. And then, pretty soon, things start to go wrong. I start thinking about the excitement of a fresh start, a new man. And it starts all over again.

DESPAIR

The stage of the addiction cycle in which remorse is experienced is the "Despair" stage. Feelings of self-worth and self-esteem are at their lowest ebb. It is at this point that an addict vows never to repeat the abusive behavior. Each time after an addict acts out, she experiences despair in the form of regret or shame. She may resolve that she will not engage in this behavior again and minimize her despair by rationalizing that her partner cannot meet her sexual desires. Eventually, she begins to pre-occupy again, the resultant excitement diminishes the despair, and the cycle is repeated.

We wish to emphasize that not all women who were sexually abused as children grow up to have a sexual addiction. Whether or not a person has an addiction needs to be decided with the help of a professional who has expertise in dealing with compulsive behaviors. A key element in identifying whether someone has a sexual addiction involves understanding the meaning of "willpower." Many recovering victims who are not addicts feel shame when being sexual, and this can be dealt with in traditional therapy. Sexual addiction is a different problem. It involves compulsively, obsessively acting out sexually; willpower cannot control it. The addict is powerless, compelled to be sexual in ways of which she is not accepting, and as a result, about which she feels shame. Sexual addiction is treatable.

If you suspect that you have a sexual addiction, seek help from a professional who understands and has had experience working with addictions. Seek information and peer support within your community. There are groups forming across the country, similar in format to Alcoholics Anonymous, which assist persons on the road to recovery.

FUNCTIONS OF ADDICTION

Why does a person become enmeshed in an addiction in the first place? What is the fatal attraction, the seductive lure? To understand addiction, consider the needs or wants that it promises to satisfy or supply.

PROMISE:
Addiction will provide you with confidence — a euphoric state of being that helps you believe that you are in control, of yourself and life.

TRUTH:
The confidence that addiction provides is false and delusionary. It is present only as long as the drug of choice is present.

PROMISE:
Addiction is a way to avoid feeling an emotion or to substitute an acceptable emotion for an unacceptable one. It is a vehicle to escape from reality, to isolate, to "drop out." When a person functions through an addiction she experiences an excitement and exhilaration she does not usually experience when sober — a "rush," a "high," a "hit."

TRUTH:
The price for attaining the state of bliss promised by addiction is the loss of one's identity. The addict must adopt a lifestyle based on denial and delusion, a state of being that requires more and stronger "hits" to maintain.

The addiction is reinforced by the addict's belief that she is achieving a valuable "payoff" or "reward." The addictive behavior becomes a much desired experience. Addiction is a rapacious master, demanding increasingly rigorous conformity from the addict to achieve satisfaction or satiation. The addict takes more and more risks to gain the desired illusions of control, the emotional highs, the escape from a reality that is painful and frightening to confront. Denial and delusion close out the real world and reinforce the vicious addiction cycle; it continues and escalates. If it is not broken, the addict is lost — to herself, to the world of sobriety, and ultimately to life.

RECOVERY FROM ADDICTION

The design and implementation of your own personal recovery program requires that you create a healthy environment for yourself — physically, psychologically and spiritually.

(1) Chart your own addiction cycle.
    a. pre-occupation
    b. ritualization
    c. acting out
    d. despair

(2) Recognize the stresses that precipitate your addictive cycle:
    a. events
    b. emotions
    c. behaviors
    d. memories
    e. other

(3) Remember and resolve childhood experiences that trigger the cycle:
    a. events
    b. relationships
    c. emotions
    d. behaviors
    e. memories
    f. other

(4) Identify your own personal strengths. Identify your own personal weaknesses.
    a. emotional
    b. mental
    c. behavioral
    d. relational
    e. other

(5) Make two charts:
   a. Describe how you feel, think and behave when you are **IN ADDICTION**.
   b. Describe how you feel, think and behave when you are **IN RECOVERY**.

(6) Decide what mental health programs can facilitate your recovery and choose to be involved in them. Your considerations should include: a Twelve Step Program similar to that of Alcoholics Anonymous, self-help groups for victims of early life trauma, and psychotherapy with a qualified therapist.

ADDICTION AND RELATIONSHIPS

Compulsive behaviors are extremely difficult issues to confront and treat, but relationships can survive and grow through constructively facing the truth. Not all relationships will survive. One partner or the other may choose not to change or grow, not to increase the commitment in the relationship, or to not increase the level of intimacy. Be an actor, not a reactor. Make a decision to move forward in your own growth process. Your partner can make the choice to move with you or to be left behind. It will be up to you to accept his position, wait for him to grow, or to move on without him.

Do not let the shame, fear, or pain of your abuse or your addiction keep you from becoming whole and healthy. Compulsivity is a learned behavioral problem that can be unlearned and replaced with nourishing habits. You have within you an indomitable spirit, your perfect and innocent child. The same strengths that facilitated your survival to this point are resources which will facilitate your successful recovery, allowing you to connect with your "self" and with healthy love relationships.

SEXUAL SABOTAGE

LORRI:

I always think that there is something wrong with me when I feel good about sex.

A person who has been sexually abused as a child makes many erroneous conclusions about the experience, and forms a belief system based on those conclusions. She believes there is something inherently wrong with her as a human being, and often believes that there is something inherently wrong with her sexuality. This belief system manifests itself in many ways — shame-based decisions, fear responses, haunting memories, avoidance of sex or compulsive involvement in sex, to name only a few examples.

CLAIRE:

I experience an overwhelming sense of shame when I feel good sexually.

Some women are able to perform physically. They may experience physical excitement or arousal. They may achieve orgasm by using fantasy or they may fake orgasm with impressive acting skills. They may still feel "empty." They may not experience emotional satisfaction. As a result, they may be turned off by the idea of being sexual with their primary partners, be indifferent towards them, or continually repeat self-defeating sexual behaviors in an attempt to find personal satisfaction or to please their partners.

LORRI:

I would go out and find somebody to hurt me. It was the only way that I could experience a physical release, an orgasm.

BECKY:

The only way I could have an orgasm was to be physically abused in the same way I was as a child.

The role of pain, humiliation, or physical abuse in sexuality is a complex and controversial subject. Faulty beliefs, cues, unresolved traumas and habitualized coping strategies enmesh some women in compulsive cycles of sexual self-abuse. The self-abuse is usually similar to the pattern of abuse that each woman experienced as a child. It is compulsive in that it is outside of the person's willpower to change — even when it is clear to her that it is not healthy. Some women describe it as suicidal in nature.

MARIE:

I would go out looking for someone to sexually use me. Somebody to beat me up, physically and emotionally. Somebody to make me feel something!

Marie's use of defense mechanisms like isolation and dissociation was chronic and extreme, and her sexual acting out was compulsive and dangerous. The most revealing part of her statement is in the last sentence. Her desire to experience feelings, to come alive and be rid of the numbness she experienced everyday of her life, was so great that she chose feeling pain over feeling nothing at all.

MARIE:

I am so ashamed of my body. I'm so embarrassed by all the scars (inflicted by her stepfather) — I'll never be able to let another man see me.

JEANIE:

When I was a kid, I did a lot of crazy things — cigarette burns, shaving my hair off, tattoos. I was really working at hurting myself, at being ugly.

When soldiers are wounded in battle, the resultant scars are perceived as badges of courage in our culture. The woman who has survived childhood sexual abuse is as much a hero. Her scars are tangible, daily reminders that she has confronted and survived life-threatening situations. They are evidence of her battle with the dark side of life. Feelings of pain and shame are often attached to acknowledging this evidence. Being free of these reactions means first working through the tragedies of the past. It is a painful process and requires courage. It is a process to be dealt with on the individual's timetable and under conditions of support and professional guidance. When a recovering victim realizes and acknowledges that she has not only survived but triumphed over the extraordinary adversities of her childhood, personal power replaces the pain and shame. The past no longer has power over her; the past empowers her.

LOIS:
I know I overeat to keep myself isolated. It's crazy because there is a part of me that wants to be attractive.

Eating disorders also sabotage sexual intimacy. Persons who were abused as children did not receive all the nurturance they needed to feel safe and loved. For them, food may become a surrogate caretaker, always dependable, always comforting, always satisfying. If a woman grew up in a family which placed a high value on food as a reward or means of getting attention, then she was set up for an adulthood of overeating in order to achieve love or self-worth.

Remember that when a child is victimized, she is not in control of her life; her abuser is. Food may become one of the only areas of her life in which she has any choices, the only place she gets to experience control. To express her rage or self-hate, she may overeat or starve herself.

The motivations behind severe eating disorders such as anorexia nervosa and bulimia nervosa are complex. They are connected to anger, pain, shame, and control. They are also motivated by resistance to maturing. The patient resists moving out of the dysfunctional role she played as a child in her family of origin. She fears the demands and responsibilities of adulthood. Severe eating disorders are life-threatening, compulsive in nature, and outside one's self-control. They require expert, professional intervention.

Scars, obesity and malnutrition all result in a loss of perceived attractiveness. Many former victims fear being perceived as sexually desirable. Remember the abused child's logic, "If I were not so pretty, this would not have happened to me." By actively marking her body with scars or tattoos, or by passively sabotaging her appearance with eating disorders, she protects herself from having to deal with the same attention which gave her so much shame, pain, or fear as a child.

Many women make themselves unattractive in more subtle ways with the messages they communicate, verbally and non-verbally. They may deliberately hide their attractiveness by dressing in an unflattering fashion and exhibiting slovenly personal habits. They may present a hostile front in order to keep people at a distance. They may act crazy or unpredictable. Profanity, sarcasm, or ridicule can be used to put people off, to end relationships. They overtly and covertly discourage anyone from finding them attractive.

BETH:
To enjoy sex, I have to be with a man who embarrasses me.

A former victim will often sabotage her chances for healthy sexuality by surrounding herself with people who give her messages that confirm her perception of herself as unattractive. She may find herself consistently in relationships with persons who ask her to perform sexual acts to which she feels an aversion. She may be attracted to people who consistently tell sexist and degrading jokes. Her sexual partners will be persons whose perception of her is as a sexual object. Many women find that they are attracted to men with qualities similar to those of the man who abused them as a child. A victim seeking to fulfill her concept of worthlessness believes that she deserves to be with persons who covertly or overtly display hostility toward her and degrade her, often in the most humiliating of terms.

CLAIRE:
When I think I'm getting real close to another person, especially a man, I find a reason to pull away—I get scared, and then I get angry, and then I go away.

JEANIE:
I protect myself from all men the same way that I protected myself from my stepfather. I hide the "real" me. I always hold something back.

Some women sabotage sexual health in more subtle ways. They may begin a relationship on good terms but arbitrarily end it when their partners show signs of wanting more intimacy and commitment. A childhood victim may be comfortable in a relationship only as long as her partner knows little about her personally. She may seek out differences and disagreements to create distance in a developing relationship. She may begin a new relationship as a means of ending a current one.

BECKY:
I back away when a man starts getting close to me. I decide that I "care too much" and I sabotage the relationship. This is a lifetime pattern.

Intimacy and commitment can be avoided by spending years waiting for "Mr. Right" to come along. For many victims, no partner is ever quite right; there is always some perceived flaw that will prevent real intimacy from occurring. To the former victim, controlled and exploited as a child, control in issues of sexuality becomes all-important.

All of the behaviors that we have described are self-abusive and self-defeating. They are avenues by which a former victim can fulfill her negative beliefs of herself. All are dysfunctional ways of dealing with powerful emotional and behavioral patterns. All serve the purpose of sabotaging the development of a healthy perspective of one's own sexuality. Dysfunctional beliefs and habitualized behavior patterns combine to block the development of a healthy love relationship.

If you are struggling with any of the above situations, or suspect that you may be, seek help from persons whom you trust. Share your feelings — the pain, the anger, the sadness, the fear. Move forward in the process of setting free the "innocent child" within you.

SEXUAL FULFILLMENT

LANA:

Intercourse isn't the problem. The problem is intimacy—it's so scary, being vulnerable with someone, risking getting hurt again.

One of the meanings of "to be sexual" is, "to relate to another person physically." You may say that is self-evident, but the ways in which a person can be sexually, physically expressive are varied. It is a subject of much controversy and aggressive debate. Much of what is commonplace sexual behavior between legally married partners is still illegal in most states. Much of what is common in alternate lifestyles is deemed immoral by large populations of people. So how do we define what is healthy sexual behavior between two adults?   With great trepidation, but here goes . . . .

First of all, it is more than the simple physical act. There are more dimensions involved if sexual expression is to be more than a recreational activity. This is not to say that sex cannot be fun or an outlet for playfulness. But for sex to be more than playfulness, it has to be experienced on more dimensions than the physical. For it to be an act of love, there has to be a mental and emotional union, a bonding between the two partners. Each partner has to be totally "present" for it to be an expression of spirit rather than just an "hormonal high." To "be present" means to be "in the moment," "to be aware," to be "tuned in" or "in tune" with yourself and with your partner. This is no small accomplishment, and many people deceive themselves into thinking they have it "all together," even as they are jumping indiscriminately from one bed to another. To have it "all together" requires a deeper commitment than is possible with only a recreational investment.

To be mentally present means to have your thoughts on your partner and the event the two of you are sharing. It means to be clear in one's mind that, "This is a person with whom I wish to be intimate." It means being clear with oneself that, "I am involved with this person to the point of commitment to something greater than my own selfish needs." It means thinking in terms of "we." It means accepting full responsibility for your own imperfections. It means accepting that your partner's imperfections are his responsibility. It means being relatively free of dysfunctional beliefs of self, relationships, and sexuality so as to be able to truly experience physical and psychological intimacy for the magnificent sharing experience that it can be. Without the above ingredients, the experience will be like two people masturbating with each other's bodies.

SEXUAL FANTASY

IMAGINATION:
The synthesis of mental images into new ideas...

PHANTASY/FANTASY:
A product of imagination... (*Psychiatric Dictionary, Fifth Edition*, Robert J. Campbell, M.D., Oxford University Press, 1981)

It is critical that mental health professionals understand the role that the habituated use of fantasy can play in sexual dysfunction. In the field of sex therapy it is generally accepted that fantasy is a useful intervention to improve sexual relationships. In the treatment of victims of sexual abuse, we have found that the use of fantasy can be detrimental and counterproductive. Remember that, for many victims, fantasizing was a way to escape from reality. When the abuse was repetitive and intense, the escape (or defense mechanism) became habituated. Some victims were tricked by their abuser into believing that what was happening was an expression of love. As adults they will fantasize that this was true. A commonly described fantasy is being with an imaginary "hero" who bears a remarkable resemblance to the victimizer.

For the woman who utilized fantasy in childhood to cope with her abuse, sexual fantasizing in adulthood will maintain a psychological and emotional barrier between herself and her partner. It may make it easier for her to perform sexually, just as it did when she was a child. It will not help her to reach a far more rewarding goal—intimacy.

Imagination and fantasy can play an important therapeutic role for persons breaking away from old patterns of behavior. However, if either partner is struggling with a sexual addiction, fantasizing will take away from the degree to which a person is mentally present with her partner. Decide for yourself, with the help of a competent professional, whether or not the use of fantasy in your sexual relationships is advisable.

> *SYLVIA:*
>
> *Fantasizing while having a sexual relationship is a way that I bypass intimacy—it's a head trip that keeps me in control and I don't lose power. If I don't establish intimacy with someone before I have sex with them, then it is only lust. Intimacy must come first before the sexual experience because my first impulse is to by-pass everything else and get sexual and convince myself that I'm in love.*

Shutting off one's feelings in order to survive a traumatic experience is a common coping mechanism. Suppressing memories or fantasizing are also used to reduce the stress of abuse. Being able to perform sexually does not by itself mean that a person is free of sexual dysfunction. Sylvia discovered that the "freedom" she had to fantasize was a way of keeping herself from being vulnerable with a partner. It was a way to avoid "being in touch" with another human being. Remember that many women who were sexually victimized as children are capable of physically performing the sexual act as adults. What is much more difficult for them is to be emotionally and mentally present while being sexual. This does not mean they are defective. It means they learned a pattern of behavior repeatedly connected with threatening situations in the past. Because the behavior was learned, it can be unlearned.

THE COMPLEXITY OF HEALTHY SEXUAL EXPRESSION

A healthy, loving sexual expression between two people is a complex biological, mental, and emotional phenomenon. Bringing all these dimensions together is not easy, and it is not something which is simply "natural." It is something which is learned with experience, knowledge, maturity and practice. Performing the "physical act" is the easiest part. The other dimensions require knowing oneself and allowing oneself to be known. Fears and shame from the past need to be resolved. The fear of intimacy has to be confronted. The process requires a partner willing to communicate, share, and self-examine. No sexual difficulty in a relationship is one

cate, share, and self-examine. No sexual difficulty in a relationship is one
partner's responsibility. The fears of sexual expression are shared and so
are the joys. The problems are shared by both partners, and the rewards
are celebrated as a couple.

It is the nature of every human being to want to be all that she is
capable of being and to make meaningful connections with other human
beings. When we are vulnerable, honest, and tender with each other,
expressing oneself sexually is a wonderful means by which a person can be
in harmony with another human being. It is a state of being that many
people never experience because of abuse, ignorance and fear.

If your sex-life is not as satisfying as you would like it to be or if
you find that you are not sexually motivated, do not despair. Victims know
better than anyone that there are times when not being sexually active is a
greater act of love than intercourse or orgasm. Sexually explicit behavior is
but one means of bridging the chasm between two people. It is but one
means of expressing love. It is but one dimension of intimacy. There may
be other issues in your recovery program to be attended to first: building
self-esteem, overcoming painful memories, learning effective parenting
skills, etc.

From time to time you will need to take a break from working a
recovery program and allow yourself to experience simply relaxing and
enjoying life. Be patient and gentle with yourself. Choosing not to be
sexually active is a reasonable option. Intimacy does not require physical
sexual expression; however, loving sexual expression does require intimacy.
Everyone has her own timetable in life. Allow yourself the option that
someday you may decide to develop an intimate, non-sexual friendship into
a healthy sexual relationship.

During moments of vulnerability, trust, and honesty, a person is
capable of sharing her innermost dimensions. The degree of intimacy each
person experiences depends upon a balance of critical factors — self-worth,
maturity, trust and compassion, to name a few. All of these factors can be
cultivated; all of them are constantly evolving and changing. It is a lifetime
process. No dimension of an intimate relationship, especially sexual expression, has to stagnate. It is constantly revitalized if both partners are constantly growing.

7

RECOVERY AND SELF-DISCOVERY

The fewer secrets that I keep in myself, the more risks I take, the more I share — the stronger I get. MARIE

INTRODUCTION

Whether you experienced years of abuse or one traumatic incident, the recovery process can often be a lengthy one. You have probably spent a significant portion of your life believing yourself to be inadequate and shameful. Give yourself some time to change what may be a lifetime of dysfunctional patterns. Be gentle and compassionate with yourself. Recognize that the coping skills you used as a child enabled you to survive. Give yourself credit for doing the best that you could with the resources that you had. Affirm each step in your journey of recovery. Every effort, no matter how small, deserves to be recognized and appreciated by you. It is a reflection of your courage and determination to know the perfect and innocent child within you.

LOUISE:
I don't ever want to forget it (the abuse) again, because now I realize that I had a whole lot of strength and courage to go through some of the things that I did. Now I am proud of myself instead of ashamed. I still rely on some of the strengths that got me through it then, like refusing to quit trying, even when my dad told me I was hopelessly incompetent. Remembering, for me, is what makes the strengths grow now.

MARIE:

*I decided a long time ago to turn the terrible things that happened
to me into something good for others. . . It's the only way I could
make sense out of it.*

A person without sight develops her other senses to a finer degree.
She distinguishes between odors, delights in the texture of a flower's petal,
and savors the sweetness of a fine chocolate. She learns to identify a
person's emotional state by the inflection of his/her voice and "sees" a
person's inner beauty through the ways in which that person treats others.
So also can a victim of childhood sexual abuse develop qualities within
herself to compensate for her deprivation. Victims know abandonment,
powerlessness, domination, exploitation, fear, and invasion of one's own
body. For the abuse victim, these words do not represent concepts discussed in textbooks, they are experiential realities.   No one can appreciate
the gifts of love and freedom more that the person who has endured their
absences and spent her life in search of them. To be truly loved and
accepted, with few demands or expectations, becomes a gift to be highly
valued and treated with reverence and appreciation.

CINDY:

*I now know that I can learn from something even as devastating as
this and still go on to bigger and better things. I know that I have
choices—I can let it (the abuse) be an albatross and drag me
down, or I can fight for myself.*

Because victims are taught in childhood to react to other people's
needs rather than their own, they often grow up to be highly sensitive and
aware people. They advocate for helpless animals, express concern for
persons in need, and identify with the powerless in society. In her recovery
program a victim learns to act rather than react, to care for herself as well
as others. A recovering victim with a growing awareness and expression of
personal power is a victim no more. Recovering victims represent a population that possesses the potential to effect significant political and social
change.

A BLUEPRINT FOR SUCCESS

LANA:

I finally realized that there was no prescription that I could take to get over it [the abuse]. I thought that there were these steps that I could go through and be "cured" afterwards. . .I learned that there is no set way, that people are different, and we get over it in different ways and on different timetables.

Education is a vital part of a recovery program. Become familiar with the terms and concepts of recovery and learn how they apply to you: belief system, defense mechanisms, shame, the person you were born to be, control, behavior patterns, compulsivity, healthy and unhealthy fears, cues, etc. Understand the prevalence of the problem of abuse, the deceptions, the secrecy, the complexities. Explore its influence in all dimensions of your life—friendships, marriage, self-concept, child-rearing, sexuality, career, parental and family relationships. Seek out knowledge from a variety of sources. Discuss the issues with friends, family, and professionals. Knowledge is power.

As you educate yourself, practice being more aware of your own behavior, thoughts, and feelings. Keep a journal. Record your thoughts, feelings, insights, memories, dreams, patterns, and successes. Recognize your preferred defense mechanisms. Identify when, where and how often during the day you experience shame, fear and pain.

Diagram and describe the belief system you established as a young child (before the age of eight to ten.) How does it influence your daily life? How does it influence your decision-making? In what ways have your beliefs become self-fulfilling prophecies? What are your methods of control? What are your sexuality or intimacy issues? What self-defeating behavior patterns do you recognize?

CINDY:

The most important thing that has happened for me is that I'm not playing the victim role anymore. I recognize it now, when I'm being a victim, and I don't fall into it as often.

One goal of recovery is freedom. The experience of freedom is power. As a person sheds her "victim mentality" she is empowered with the freedom to choose. She is empowered with the joy of discovering herself. She is empowered with the ability to love herself and to be intimate with others. Freedom is the willingness to make decisions. Maturity is the willingness to take responsibility for those decisions. What are some decisions you need to make? What are some immediate actions you can take? What are some possible goals? Decide which issues are the most difficult to face and which are the most approachable. Let the first steps be those in which you feel the greatest confidence and ones that will ensure the most success. A progression of small successes will build confidence. Tackling the toughest issues first can be a setup for failure.

CINDY:
Sometimes I still play the victim role, but it is harder to do when I check out my reality and let myself "feel."

Sometimes you will fall short of your expectations as you clear away the psychological debris from your childhood. Progress will sometimes be two steps forward and one step backwards. But unless you live your life "as if" all things are possible, unless you live your life "as if" you deserve joy and serenity, you will never discover how far you could have gone on your journey of self-discovery.

CLAIRE:
When I first came for counseling, I had no self-esteem, no self-respect, and no self-worth. Now, although it's a daily effort and I still fall back sometimes, I'm starting to love myself.

Accept the "innocence of childhood" as a truth for all persons, including yourself. Remember that the child that was hurt in those early years still resides within you. She needs the love, attention and protection she never experienced. In therapy and on your own, practice imagining her with you now. Acknowledge to your child that you know how she thinks and feels. Let her know that she is no longer alone; you are with her. Embrace her, when you are ready. Believe that no one is born shameful, bad, dirty, or morally defective. Each person's behavior is understandable when one considers the biological equipment she was born with and the environment in which she was forced to cope and attempt to meet her needs. Believe that every child deserves the experience of happiness.

After you make the decision to pursue a recovery program, take the time to plan your strategy. A support system will be vital. Check out local support groups, churches, social service agencies, and professionals. Trust your instincts. If a person or a group does not feel right for you, try another. A support system can include family and old friends, but remember that some of them may have also been part of the problem. Challenge yourself as to whether they are affirming your recovery or still operating in old or dysfunctional patterns.

Be wary of persons who deny your reality, what you believe to be true. Some will fear your story; some will discount its influence; some will be threatened by your strength; some will wonder if they would have had the same capabilities in your situation. Those who cast doubt on you and your reality are the ones who doubt themselves the most.

Be aware that as you grow, many of your relationships will change. Those individuals who are willing and able will grow with you. Those persons who do not want you, your relationship with them, or themselves, to change will oppose you. Do not let them stop your progress. If you can accept them as they are, celebrate that fact. If you cannot, let them go and continue on your road to health. Some people will leave you, and you will let go of some people. As you practice living in recovery, you will develop a discerning eye for which relationships are most healthy.

As your best friend, partner, or spouse supports you in your healing process, a time will come when the roles will be reversed. You can best love your partner at that time by being supportive of him as he faces his own issues. Use loving confrontation when needed. You have stepped from the darkness into the light. There will be times when you will be asked to step back into the dark and give a hand to someone there who is looking for guidance.

LANA:
Pointing out my strengths was very important. Whenever I was
feeling particularly alone or overcome by this terrible thing that had

happened to me and someone would say, "You are really strong,
I'm honored to be with someone who has so much strength and
has come this far,". . .that would give me courage to go on.

There is a power about people who return from battle, veterans who have looked into the face of death and destruction and survived. Persons who have not been tested in such a manner stand in awe of these warriors. Others sometimes fear what they themselves have not experienced and do not understand. The power that comes from over-coming adversity is a strength that every recovering victim can cultivate within herself.

LORRI:

I'm always worrying about whether the way that I behave now, the
things I do, are because of the incest or because they are just a
normal part of me. It's such a relief when I find out I'm normal.

At some time in each person's program, we recommend that she be involved with activities or groups which are not abuse-oriented. The reasons for this are two: (1) She needs not to get caught in the pattern of identifying herself solely as a victim; and (2) She needs to learn that many of the issues she is facing in life are common to all women and not the result of childhood sexual abuse. It is important to learn which struggles in life are abuse-connected and which are "normal" struggles, endemic to all persons. The ability to make this distinction will be of great value to you.

LANA:

I have put it (the abuse) into perspective as being a part of my life
experience, like a handicap—something I must learn to deal with.

JEANIE:

I have learned that every victim has her own experience, and her
recovery program must be tailored to her specific and personal
needs.

The definition of success and recovery is specific to each individual. Encourage yourself to stretch, but also be practical. You have had years of practice in your current patterns. Allow yourself realistic expectations. Allow for the unexpected. Be gentle with yourself. Utilize rest periods or vacations. Make a commitment to yourself. It can be time-involvement, an issue resolved, an educational goal realized. Recognize that you will experience resistance within yourself. Old behaviors and attitudes will resist being extinguished. Be patient but determined. Initially the new approaches will feel awkward and require much conscious effort. With time they will become more comfortable and you will be more confident. Fulfill your commitments and celebrate your accomplishments. Every goal realized deserves celebration; it is a vital part of coming alive.

OVERCOMING SHAME

FRAN:
I know the patterns that I want to change in myself; they are the ones that make me be so hard on myself because I feel worthless and shameful.

Earlier in the book we identified shame as a feeling which is "passed on" by people who dwell in that feeling and carry it with them. Continue to conceptualize shame in this manner. Shame is deceptive and confusing. It does not belong to you. It is not about you. It is about the person or persons who shamed you. It belongs to them. You were not born shameful. Feelings of shame were imposed on you by others using psychological and physical abuse. It has nothing to do with your spiritual being. Shame is a destructive and cruel delusion passed on by persons who are themselves infected by it.

"Shaming" is a form of psychological abuse endemic to parent-child relationships. It is often transmitted by well-intentioned persons who are attempting to express caring and love. They received the shame in much the same manner as they now pass it on to you. Acknowledging that the sources of your shame were parents or caretakers does not mean that you are blaming or condemning them. It means that you are placing responsibility where it belongs. Often it was a well-intentioned relative who shamed you. You no longer need to protect their feelings or make excuses for them. They, like us, must be allowed the responsibility for their weaknesses as well as their strengths. "Giving back the shame" is a critical step in the process of breaking the bonds of shame. It is possible to ritualize, in a therapeutic setting, the process of "giving back the shame" to the person(s) who gave it to you. This can be done effectively in the absence of the shaming person by imagining that he/she is present.

CINDY:
Probably the most important thing that has happened for me is that I'm not playing the victim role anymore.

Remember that you were born perfect and innocent. If you were a victim of childhood sexual abuse, you can be handicapped by faulty beliefs, habitualized fear responses, and compulsive patterns of self-defeating behavior. You can confront and conquer these issues. You are not your actions. You are not your habits. You are not your beliefs. You are much more—a being of untapped and mysterious potential. You can break the bonds of shame and set yourself free.

It may be necessary to feel anger for a time toward the person(s) who gave you their shame. Healthy anger, what we call "righteous anger," can provide the strength to help you keep in perspective that the shame of your abuse is another person's responsibility, that it does not belong to you. It can help you decide to no longer carry the shame for someone else.

Freeing oneself of shame and shame-based responses is an ongoing process. It will be necessary to periodically reaffirm your decision not to handicap yourself with shame. There will be times when it will sneak back into power in your life. This may occur during periods of sadness and pain or even at times when you are experiencing happiness and success.

The recurrence of shame does not mean that you are failing in your recovery program. It means that you are human. Be patient and gentle with yourself. Shame is a wily adversary. To defeat it requires a determination to battle it as long as necessary to free yourself of its power. You can learn to recognize when it is beginning to insinuate itself back into your life. Notice when you are apologizing unnecessarily, discounting your sense of reality, and sabotaging your own happiness. These are warning signals that shame would like to find a home with you again. How many other shame-based behaviors and attitudes can you identify?

LANA:

When I used to talk about my abuse, I felt like I was talking about somebody else. Now when I talk about it, I'm talking about me, and I know that I'm O.K.

Do not despair in the persistence of long-established behavior patterns such as shame. You have spent much of your life unaware of your own power and potential. You could not confront what you were unable to see. Now you are seeing with increasing clarity. Be specific in your description of what you want to be different in your life. What are the habits, patterns, cues, beliefs, or defense mechanisms that you want to change? Define what you want in specific terms. If asking politely for support from others is ineffective, then demand vigorously. You have a right to be healthy.

HELEN:

I have put my abuse into perspective. . .it is part of me, not all of me. It is not a shameful secret, but something that I can accept and deal with, like blindness or diabetes or a broken arm.

Reconnecting with and accepting one's inner child is a vital part of healing. Many women separate emotionally from all or part of their childhood as a means of coping. But denying part of your life means separating from the good, as well as bad; it means separating from reality. It is important that you learn how to love yourself in the present, and to love the innocent child within you. She needs the love, attention, and protection she never experienced. In therapy and on you own, imagine her with you. Embrace her. Acknowledge to your child that you know how she thinks and feels. Let her know she is no longer alone; you are with her. Let her know that you will protect and cherish her, that she is finally safe and loved.

JEANIE:
I know now that the abuse is not me, it is something that was done to me.

It is vital in the recovery process to separate your own identity from that of the abuser. This is the process of "individuation"—recognizing yourself as being a distinct and unique being who is responsible for her own behavior and attitudes; deciding that you are not responsible for the feelings and behaviors resulting from another person's actions.

RECOGNIZING THE TRUTH OF THE PAST

Recognizing the "reality" of your childhood—the truth about what the past was really like—facilitates the process of identifying the abusive, destructive and detrimental attitudes and behaviors that belong to that time period. Victims need to learn and believe, "That was then and this is now. I am no longer a child controlled by adults; I am an adult woman capable of controlling myself." When issues are not identified and confronted, problems are generalized and scattered throughout one's life experiences in disguise, unfairly tainting what should be positive and healthy experiences. For example, if a child was traumatically abused by a man with red hair and the resulting pain and fear were never acknowledged or resolved, she might, as an adult, generalize her negative feelings to all men with red hair.

A husband and wife who are clients of ours once expressed great frustration with a bitter Sunday morning fight. The resulting depression and hurt seemed out of proportion to the apparent issues. The couple had just experienced a wonderful week together, a time of closeness and sharing. During careful examination of their behavior, thoughts and feelings just prior to the argument, the wife recalled a fear response to her husband as he dressed in a white shirt and dark suit in preparation for church. She was able to identify this as a cue from the past. Her husband had dressed in much the same manner as her father had done when he was preparing for church. Her father had severely abused her when she was a child, often just before leaving for church. The wife found herself reacting to her husband with anger and fear, but without awareness of why she felt such extreme pain.

The real issue was not between her and her husband at all. It was between her and her father. Her abusive father was the source of her emotional responses, not her husband. Through therapy she learned how to identify, separate out, and deal with the feelings she had towards her father. She now "sees" her husband as someone different and separate from her abuser. She has separated the feelings from the present and returned them to the issues of her past, where they belong. She is learning that she is much more than an abused child of questionable worth. She is becoming free to recognize and to celebrate the intimacy and successes in her marriage.

SUCCESS

IRENE:
It's kinda strange. Today, coming to group, I thought that maybe I'd just walk in and tell you all that I had just been making up stories. I know that there are times that I wish it just hadn't happened.

Many clients describe the recovery process as a combination of joy and fear. The joy is felt in response to an increasing awareness of "self" and the resultant freedom, love, and personal power. The fear is about the unknown and all the life changes that are required. Sometimes life may seem too good to be true, too good to be trusted, too good to cope with emotionally. The sadness is felt when a recovering victim reflects on the time in her life that has been wasted in dysfunctional behaviors and thoughts. She remembers failed relationships and missed opportunities, and laments, "If only I had known then what I know now, so many of my problems could have been avoided."

It is appropriate for a person to go through a grieving process as part of her recovery program. Grieving is not to be confused with depression or thoughts of failure, self-defeat, or self-destruction. It is a genuine mourning for the death of the "old you." A goal of the grieving process is to "let go of" the person you used to be. Grieving the changes and loss of your old self may feel like the death of an old and familiar friend, a friend who had been outgrown and left behind as you moved forward in life.

Acknowledging the pain and sadness and feeling it for a period of time may be necessary. You can facilitate this part of the healing process by writing about the "old you," looking through old photographs, or reflecting on a favorite keepsake. Ritualize the experience. Say good-bye to the "old you" and embrace the "new you." Forgive yourself for mistakes that you made, for not knowing everything you needed to be healthy, and that you missed opportunities to deal with certain problems. Actually saying good-bye verbally and ritually putting closure on the "old you" can help you define the end of counterproductive times and the beginning of new perspectives. Ritualizing the "new you" can help make it real also. Moving into a new home, starting a new career, making new friends, going back to school, setting realistic goals and working toward achieving them, are all ways of actualizing your new lifestyle.

CRISIS

Recovery involves emotional conflict and crisis. A person who experiences no conflict in life is either comatose or dead. Recovery involves allowing yourself to feel a wide range of emotions, including fear, pain, guilt and anger. It means experiencing and accepting joy, love, and growing self-esteem.

You can decide to treat a crisis as an enemy, as something that is dangerous. You can avoid, deny or magnify it. You can label it setback or catastrophe. You can bemoan your misfortune, complain about the unfairness of life, attack perceived enemies, surrender to fate and indulge in marathon pity-parties. Or you can take control. You can choose to view a crisis as an opportunity. You can solicit trustworthy advice, build and resource a support system, seek pertinent information, restore yourself through prayer and meditation, engage in therapy, and allow yourself to experience the love of others. You can be empowered.

It is important that you acknowledge, to yourself and to significant others, the times when you take emotional and behavioral risks. It is equally important to communicate your joy and sense of accomplishment when you experience success. Asking a friend not to speak loudly at the library may be a big emotional risk for you; you may fear her rejection and ridicule. Asking her to speak more softly requires behaving assertively. Letting her know how you feel about your behavior means modeling honesty and vulnerability.

NEW REALITIES

BARBARA:

My advice to others is to pay attention to your own reactions. When you catch yourself reacting like a victim, such as isolating, say to yourself, "I'm going to do something different this time."

The attractive influence of the familiar cannot be overestimated. A lifetime of experiences, a strong set of core beliefs, and fear keep people enmeshed in counterproductive patterns of reacting to life. Perhaps when a child was vulnerable, people took advantage of her. When she was happy or playful, she was shamed. She learned to suppress within herself those experiences which signify joy. She learned to always be on guard and to prepare for the unexpected. It is quite logical that such experiences cause people to mistrust love and happiness.

A child victim develops an adult pattern of mistrusting "good" feelings or situations. She looks for "the catch" if whatever is happening appears to be good. She wonders what other persons might be "up to." She begins to imagine what might "really" be going on. She may take control of the situation by ending the "good" feelings with something she says or does. She may precipitate a conflict and then feel justified in withdrawing, emotionally and/or physically.

When a child grows up with exploitation, violence, and sexual abuse, she learns to mistrust all people, and to misunderstand and fear gentle, caring, and loving people. She fears them because she believes that "everybody is after something." She attacks them because she experiences shame in their presence; she does not believe herself to be "as good as" they are. Do not let yourself be deceived or cheated by old patterns that

you were taught as a child. Courageously move towards what you perceive
as good and healthy behaviors and attitudes and nourish them as part of
your new reality.

NEW PERSPECTIVES

When a person has a physical ailment or disability, there is no
shame in any compensation or accommodation she must make for it. If a
childhood disease leaves you with a weak heart, it makes perfect sense to
do whatever is necessary to accommodate or correct the problem. Our
society is full of people accommodating various differences in physical
functioning.

The woman who was abused as a child has a similar difficulty to
accommodate or overcome. If she is afraid of the dark she can practice
taking control by having a light on at night. If she fears that her privacy
will be invaded, she can put a lock on her bedroom door. She may need to
ask herself and trusted others whether or not any of the accommodations
she makes interfere with her quality of life. If she decides to confront her
fears, she can decrease their influence over her.

IRENE:
I'm not as scared of the dark now, because now I know why
I was scared.

When a woman seeks an evaluation of her physical health, there
are a number of dimensions from which to draw her data: respiratory,
circulatory, endocrine, muscle tone, etc. An evaluation of one's psychological functioning also contains many dimensions. The text contains many
tools to be utilized in compiling a self-inventory: identifying your defense
mechanisms, understanding your belief system, recognizing cues connected
to the past, learning new patterns of behavior, etc. None of these dimensions is exclusive of the others. There are many ways in which they overlap. Decide which concepts apply to you, which ones you want to eliminate
or change, which ones you want to gain and strengthen.

CONTENT VS. PROCESS

In identifying your own patterns of behavior, it is helpful to understand the difference between content observations and process observations. Content pertains to "what" is being dealt with; it is the subject. Process pertains to "how" the subject is approached.

If you were consistently in conflict with a particular person, it would be to your advantage to analyze the situation as to content and process and to identify a pattern of behavior which could be changed. A content observation of a situation would ask, "What is it we constantly disagree about?" or "What is the subject at the root of this conflict?" A process observation would ask, "How do we go about disagreeing?" or "What is it we do that causes the conflict to continue?" Perhaps the manner in which the two of you interact is the problem rather than any specific subject.

EXAMPLE: Janet finds herself consistently running into problems in dealing with the chairperson of a committee at the church of which she is a member. Initially she decides that they have a fundamental difference of philosophy which will never be bridged. After examining the dynamics of the many disagreeable exchanges, however, Janet realizes that it is the manner in which the chairperson addresses her to which she responds with intense dislike. The content of their disagreements is not the real issue. The barrier to communicating in a positive way, from Janet's perspective, is the perceived condescending behavior of the chairperson.

Learning how to discriminate between content and process can help you identify more accurately the sources of problematic patterns of behavior. Be aware of, and ask for, feedback on your own behavior in situations — tone of voice, choice of words, posture, cues, defensiveness, etc.. Do you communicate mixed messages? Do you experience ambivalent feelings about the subject of the conflict? Do some journaling on the subject. Identify when you have felt similar feelings and under what circumstances. Has this conflict happened before with someone else? Do you see a similar or familiar pattern to other areas of your life? Self-appraisal is an opportunity to learn. Is the problem victimization, a battle worth engaging in, or something that can be easily rectified with objective changes?

THE "TRY HARDER" FALLACY

Careful analysis and new perspectives can help one avoid a trap too many people fall into in daily life — the "Try Harder" Fallacy. When a person persists in seeing a problem or situation from a particular perspective and continues to use the same methods for dealing with it, she is not changing strategy, she is increasing the effort put into the same strategy. She believes that more effort with the same strategy can bring new results to an old problem. "Trying harder" is a problem-solving approach that seldom works.

In order not to get caught up in the try harder fallacy — using the same ineffective strategy, only using it more intensely — a person must be willing to look at the possibility that what she believes to be true or real may be a deception, even a self-deception. She must be willing to believe that: (1) She was born innocent and shame-free, (2) She deserves happiness and peace of mind, and (3) She has a right, even a duty, to herself to grow and protect her growth from anyone who seeks to deny her growth and her reality.

An example of a common "try harder" fallacy statement is: "If I could just get my partner to change, then I would feel better." This statement has important implications. It says that the speaker's internal state is dependent upon an external factor, a factor that is outside the speaker's control. It therefore implies that the speaker is powerless. It is a generally accepted rule of psychology that a person who has something that another person wants has the power in the dyad. Someone caught in the "try harder fallacy" would continually conflict with her partner in an attempt to make him understand and change. Choosing to be enmeshed in this pattern or process means giving up control to another person — the one who has something that you want — your partner. As long as your partner fails to hear you or change, you are reacting rather than acting.

Therapist Earnie Larsen succinctly states, "If nothing is different, then nothing will be different." When you find yourself falling into old patterns of behavior, do something different. Persistence in a new behavior or attitude means that others can then choose to change or not change. To begin a new pattern of relating, take the risk of telling your partner that so far you have attempted to change the dynamics between the two of you without success. Explain further that you have decided not to participate in the interaction as you have in the past. You are going to try something different, and you are asking him to participate with you in the new behavior.

There may be times when you will need therapeutic help to extinguish the strong emotional response you experience being around a certain person or persons. People do not, under most circumstances, have physical and psychological control over us unless we give that control to them. The phrase "under most circumstances" is included because there are situations of extreme danger when persons of evil intent do dominate others, physically and psychologically.

In most problematic interactions, the person being confronted will resist changing. If they choose not to change, you must then decide what your response will be. Will you withdraw, tolerate, or choose another strategy? Whatever you choose to do can be done in an honest and non-shaming manner. The important part is that you assume the responsibility of deciding for you, and make a choice about your own part in the issues. Remember that doing nothing is also a choice. Taking responsibility for our decisions and acting on them is a seminal component of the maturation process — of growing up.

SPIRITUAL ABUSE

MARIE:
I didn't believe in God, because if there was a God, He wouldn't have allowed all those bad things to happen to me. But if there was a God, I was really angry at him for letting it happen, and I didn't want anything to do with him.

A person's spirituality can be a source of great strength and comfort in all areas of her life. In the course of our careers, we have provided therapy to persons from a wide spectrum of religious orientations. Each client is provided therapeutic assistance compatible with her religious orientation—Catholic, Jewish, Mormon, Presbyterian, Baptist, Native American, Methodist, or agnostic, to name only a few. The contents of this text are presented in the same broad perspective; no specific faith or concept of spirituality is advocated. We encourage you to integrate the information presented into your own particular faith or philosophy.

Those references to "spirit" in the text reflect the writers' beliefs that human beings are more than biological packages of flesh and bones, that human beings possess an additional component of humanity—call it spirit, soul, consciousness or creative energy. The references and quotes of clients reflect the clients' means of self-expression and their interpretations of their own unique experiences. Whatever one's spiritual or philosophical orientation, it is our experience that sexual abuse can profoundly influence one's belief or disbelief in God or gods.

JOYCE:

How I wanted everybody in the world to walk in that door and catch my dad hurting me! He never went to church. . .he sent us kids. God was for children.

The effect of childhood sexual abuse on a child's conceptualization of a higher power can be profound and long-lasting. The concept of God most often introduced to children is that of an entity that is all-powerful and all-knowing, a father figure (or at least a parental figure). The child accepts this simple concept. As she matures intellectually, this concept may be outgrown in some ways or replaced with a more complex and mature concept of God, but for most persons the first lessons in spirituality remain the foundation of his or her religious beliefs.

BONNIE:

I knew how my life was supposed to be, where I came from, what I was supposed to do, where I was going. Everyone in our church thought my dad was a wonderful person. In our church we believe

*that the father in the family can speak for God. What kept me in
so much turmoil was that for all that time my dad was sexually
abusing me and my sister.*

Spiritual maturation can be seriously arrested, sabotaged, or
destroyed by sexual abuse. Based on personal experience, not philosophy, victims challenge the existence of a higher power with the following queries:

If God is so powerful, why didn't He save me?

Why would God let horrible things happen to an innocent child?

Too often the conclusions that are made are:

*There must be something wrong with me, (i.e., I must be shameful) or
God would not have let this happen to me.*

*Church is for normal (i.e., shame-free) people. Nobody could love me,
not even God.*

BONNIE:
*Everybody tells me how wonderful my dad is. He's a leader in the
church and a successful and respected businessman. So there must
be something wrong with me.*

Imagine the conclusions that a child might make who is told that
God is a loving father when, at the same time, she is being sexually
exploited by her own father. Imagine the pain of a child who believes she
is so defective or damaged that even God cannot love her. Imagine the
fear of a child who is abused by a male and has been taught that God is
masculine in nature. Imagine the shame of the abused child who is taught
that people go to hell for so-called sinful behaviors in which they have
participated. Imagine the sense of alienation that a victim experiences
when asked to have faith in an unseen entity who, in her mind, did not

protect her from being sexually abused. If she is convinced that even God has abandoned her, how can she have faith in mere mortals Sexual abuse can destroy a victim's trust in her sense of reality, she may despair of ever being loved by anyone — even God.

Many children are cheated out of their spirituality by exploitation, and the resulting shame. The shameful conclusions that a child victim makes about herself and others becomes a barrier between the child and her "higher power." She is deprived of the opportunity to experience a nurturing and uplifting spiritual dimension in her life. For the spiritually abused child, religion becomes another method that adults use to control children.

Some victims may have had a single bad experience involving spirituality. At the other end of the continuum are those persons who wrestle with more complicated issues such as the role of the church as an institution, the existence or nonexistence of an omniscient God, and the power and impotence of good and evil.

In the process of coping with the abuse while it is occurring and later in a recovery program, many women find solace and strength in their religious beliefs. Others reject them altogether. Most experience at least some confusion. Ultimately, each person must find her own answers to her own spiritual issues. Our primary therapeutic concern is: if you were a victim of spiritual abuse, recognize that it was your abuser's behavior which drove the first wedge between you and your god. When you realize that you were spiritually abused by a person or persons, and not by God, you will free yourself to be available for reconciliation between you and your "higher power." Your "higher power" will be an ally, not an adversary.

HELPING OTHERS

MARIE:
I decided to take what had happened to me (the abuse) and make something positive out of it. I can help other abused children overcome their childhood traumas with what I have learned in my own recovery.

A large percentage of former victims choose, as a part of their recovery programs, to pursue some activity or profession which deals with sex education, the prevention of sexual abuse, or assisting other victims of abuse. These are valuable and much needed services, and there can be added benefit in the delivery of these services if they are provided by persons who know from a personal perspective how to empathize and facilitate healing for others. There are a variety of ways in which recovered victims can be of help: educating the public and professionals, facilitating prevention programs for children and self-help groups for victims, advocating for political action, and working in one of the "helping" professions such as social work, medicine and psychology.

The sexual abuse of one person, a child, by another person, an adult, is a tragic and irresponsible behavior. Dealing with sexual abuse, whether as a volunteer or as a professional, can invoke incredible mental and emotional strain. Even among those who are well prepared, there is a high burn-out rate and regular challenges and controversy. Sometimes a woman will assume the role of helping others before she has successfully confronted her own traumas. Frequently a woman will immerse herself in helping others to the extent that she successfully avoids dealing with her own issues. It is all to easy to fall into the trap described in a quote by statesman Adlai Stevenson: "It is often easier to fight for one's principles than to live up to them."

Daily confrontation of sexual abuse issues can exacerbate the mental and emotional weaknesses with which a recovering victim may still be struggling. Buried memories and emotions may surface and require resolution. A person dealing with sexual abuse on a regular basis needs to protect her own mental health by continually processing her experiences with trusted others, working through any emotional issues that may surface, and celebrating successes, no matter how small. If you were a victim of childhood sexual abuse and wish to be an advocate for victims, it is absolutely essential that you continue to work your own recovery program.

Following are a number of questions you should ask yourself before making a commitment to working with sexual abuse victims:

(1) What sexual abuse issues of my own have I resolved? What sexual abuse issues do I still need to work on?

(2) Have I made a commitment to my own continuing recovery program? What steps I have taken to actualize my program?

(3) From whom do I receive feedback on my progress? What do the members of my support groups say about my being a resource for other victims?

4) Would I be most effective in face-to-face involvement with victims or are there other levels where I would be more effective?

(5) Am I in touch with my feelings? Do my feelings interfere with my effectiveness as a helper?

(6) How angry am I? How much do I project my issues onto others in my therapy or growth group? In any group?

(7) Am I in denial or delusion? How much of the advice that I give others do I take for myself?

(8) Is the subject of sexual abuse the focus of my life to the extent that it excludes time and availability for intimate relationships?

(9) Do I have addiction issues of my own that need to be confronted? Issues of co-dependency?

(10) Why do I want to work with the subject of sexual abuse? Are my motives genuine?

Examine this list of questions carefully. Spend time rigorously challenging your responses. Seek the advice of persons whom you trust and respect. Consider more than one possible area of activity in which you might be effectively involved. Not everyone needs to be in person-to-person involvement. Political and social change are important and influential arenas in which to be active. Education is the basis of change and the hope for the future.

Spend time with yourself at a deep level of self-examination and honesty before committing yourself to any action. If you then decide to devote a portion of your time to making a difference in the field of sexual abuse, go for it with all the energy and enthusiasm that you possess. With all its pitfalls, strains, and challenges, it is also an area of endeavor where a person can demonstrate genuine nurturing and other-centeredness. Only when you have recognized your own abuse and defined your own recovery program are you qualified to help others on the same healing journey. Then you are ready to unite with others to achieve a goal of incontrovertible significance — the right of all children to grow up to be the persons God created them to be!

FAMILY & FRIENDS

CLAIRE:
When I told my family the truth about the abuse I wanted them to say, "I love you; I support you; I believe you." But what I needed was for it to no longer be a secret. Secrets keep shame alive. I have learned that the more I tell the truth, the more I want to live.

Perhaps you were the victim of childhood sexual abuse and never told anyone. Perhaps when you tried to tell someone, no one heard you. Perhaps when you told someone they responded by advising you to forget the past and move on with your life. Most victims are taught that keeping the secrets of the family and preserving harmony within the family system are of the highest priority. "Honor thy father and thy mother" is a maxim that is often used to justify and maintain continued secrecy in dysfunctional family systems.

The Fourth Commandment is misused by persons dedicated to maintaining the status quo. It is misused to shame you and other family victims into keeping family secrets and to sabotage the efforts of family members who attempt to discover truth and reality. Some of the overt and covert messages to maintain family secrets are: "Blood is thicker than water."; "The family takes care of its own problems."; "We don't air our dirty linen in public."; "Do nothing to upset your father and mother's perceptions of reality."; "Your mother and father are too old (or sick or fragile) to change."; "Do not burden them with your problems."; "Do not accuse them of failure. They did the best they could." You are being asked not to hold them responsible for their behavior.

Recovery involves:

(1) Recognizing and grieving for the losses of your childhood.

(2) Recovering, affirming and nurturing the innocent child within you who was abused.

(3) Acknowledging the mixture of feelings—pain, fear, sadness, anger—that you feel for parents and family members who were ineffective, neglectful or abusive.

Whether you confront your family and family friends face-to-face or symbolically is your decision. It is not necessary to confront family members face-to-face with the ways they may have failed you in life to set yourself free from the past. It is necessary that you acknowledge to yourself the ways in which your family, your primary caretakers as a child, have failed you. If your abuse has been a shameful secret in your family, then whether you have realized it or not, you have been handicapped since childhood.

You may choose to confront some family members face-to-face. Others may be deceased or no longer in your life. You can address them in a therapeutic setting using symbolic rather than actual persons. This modality may be one that you choose to use with living family members as well. One of the ways that some women choose to communicate to family members about their childhood abuse is by writing it down in a letter. There is something about seeing one's convictions and thoughts in writing that makes them real and lasting. Perhaps you are concerned that you may not be able to adequately or accurately talk about your abuse without becoming confused or shameful. Writing it down, along with any other messages you wish to communicate, is an alternative or addition to face-to-face sharing. Before you give your letter or letters to family members, you might want to share what you have written with a trusted friend or therapist and ask them if they believe the letter to be appropriate. In this way you are taking care of yourself and being fair and accurate in your communications. Written with love and honesty, a letter can be both affirming of the writer and considerate of the reader.

The following letters are edited versions of letters that Claire wrote to members of her family.

Dear Mom,

This is one of the most difficult letters I have ever had to write. I have given it a great deal of thought and meditation, and I believe it is also one of the most important letters I have ever written. There are important things that I want to say to you, and the written word seems more powerful, and clear, than any other way. Many, many words have been said in the last few months about my childhood and my abuse, or more exactly, the abuse in our family. Many, many more words have not been said. Some of them may need to be, at some time, and some of them do not. Many communications go thru three or more persons before they eventually get back to the person that they are about or who said them in the first place. Much is misunderstood, much is feared, much is frightening and painful. I want to add some clarity to this whole issue. Hopefully, eventually something good will come from it all.

First of all, I want to tell you how much I love you and how important you have been in my life, especially my childhood. I have many memories of love and communication and caring from you. I will always be grateful for these, and I believe that they gave me much of the talent and love that I have today. Thank you, Mom, for all of these.

I also want to tell you that many, many painful and abusive things were done to me by my father. I have worked long and hard in therapy to overcome the abuse in my childhood, and to live and thrive in the present and the future. It is not an easy task. I still have many things to work out and overcome. Most of the time I am determined to be all that I can be. Sometimes I am enmeshed in the past. It haunts me still, and would twist me inside out if I let it. It is a daily, an hourly struggle.

One of the most painful struggles in my life at the present involves letting go of taking care of your feelings, of protecting you. To accomplish this goal I must tell you some important things. You may choose at this point to tear this letter up, to not read any further. That is a choice you can make. My hope is that you will continue to read, even though it may be difficult to do so.

I have not lied about anything I have said about my abuse and my experiences and what I observed as a child and young person. As difficult as it is for you to believe some things, they are true. I am not crazy in the sense that I do not know reality, and no one is influencing me to be anything but truthful. I know how painful it is for you to hear some of this. I know that you find it difficult to believe or understand how you could have not known, or not seen, and why I did not tell you. I can only respond that everything that happened in our family has happened in other families and was just as unbelievable and incredible and painful. It is, however, understandable when you know more about abuse and the psychology of how people cope with trauma and stress.

You have a choice, Mom. You can choose to not believe me and to believe in a mirage, a world that didn't exist except by keeping the truth a secret. Or you can choose to believe what I say, that it did happen and that we can all deal with it, that you can deal with it, if you want to.

I have no need to do any psychological work with you personally, no need to tell you painful details or secrets. But I do need to be truthful and live a life where I can say, "It happened and I'm O.K. It happened and I was hurt very badly, but I am healing. I am living in recovery and life is worth living." I intend to keep working on my problems, I intend to work for my family to be healthy. I believe in the therapeutic process, and will live my life

*by it, to the best of my ability. If you cannot support my recovery,
if you do not believe me, and in me, then I will be healthier if I do
not see or communicate with you. I hope that this is not the way
that it must be, but I know that I must do what I believe, and you
must do the same.*

*Believe that I love you and wish all good things for you.
Believe also that I love myself and wish good things for me,
and that means living in the light, not afraid of the past.*

*With love,
Claire*

Dear Brother,

*I am writing this letter because I have some important things
that I want to tell you. The written word, I believe, has a power
different than the spoken — it is there for everyone or anyone to see,
a testament we are accountable for.*

*First, I want to tell you that I love you. I have loved you for a
long time, ever since I first saw you brought home from the hospital, a tiny, squalling bundle. That love has grown as we grew as
brother and sister. You were a brave little boy — your courage
seemed bigger than you did physically. I was proud of you as you
grew to adulthood. I was proud of you when you went to Vietnam
because you believed that it was your duty to serve your country. I
was proud of you when you became a husband and a father. I am
proud of you as you have loved and guided your children to adulthood. I wish for you happiness and fulfillment in life. I believe
that you deserve them.*

*Some of what I want to say is painful. You may not want to hear it.
I hope that you will listen. We grew up together in an abusive
family. Each of us was hurt in different ways. For a long time I
blocked out of my mind the ways in which I was abused by our
father. I believed that I was protecting Mom and the family. I
believed that I could forget and create a make-believe life. "The
past is the past and let's live in the present," kind of reasoning. I*

have learned that it's not that easy. I have learned that, for me, I must live in truth as best I can. I cannot keep secrets and pretend. I have made many mistakes in my life and I have struggled and been in great pain and fear. I have believed that I was a bad person and did not deserve to be happy. Like all abused children, I believed that I was responsible for the abuse. A long journey through therapy and some wonderful and wise people have shown me differently. I am now working to be well, to be real, to grow and share my life and love with others. To do this I must be honest. This does not mean at the expense of others. It means in a responsible, loving way.

I do not want to lose my brother. If I can do anything to help us understand and support each other, please tell me. I love you, and I am working on loving me, as I know so well that there is no hope without self-love. We were hurt a lot in our family of origin. We also learned to love each other and support each other. I want the next generation in our family to experience life without the fear and pain that we had. We can break the cycle. Love can win.

If you are still reading, thank you for trusting me. Thank you for your courage and love.

With love,
Claire

Dear Sister,

I am writing this letter because it seems like the communications system in our family often works in very strange ways. Things are said to one person, and then "get back" to someone else in the family through two or three sources, and what is really going on is anybody's guess. It seemed to me that a clearer way might be the written word.

There are some important things that I want to tell you, and I want very much to communicate them in a way that will be heard and understood. These are difficult subjects. It may be painful or difficult for you to read them. You may choose to put this letter down and not read it. I hope that you will choose to read it. I hope that you will understand it. But the choice is yours.

First I want to tell you that I love you very much. I am sorry that we did not have the chance to grow up together. We never really got to be "sisters." Now we are adults and busy, each of us, with all the interests and demands of our separate lives. We missed each other, in life's plan. I wish that we could go back and somehow magically make it different. Since we can't, I am going to attempt to make our relationship better now.

I know that I have often confused and angered you with my behavior. I know that you have often felt on the outside of "whatever" was going on, with me and with my attitude towards our family of origin. I know now that a great part of my behavior was the result of my severe abuse as a child and young person. None of this was in any way your fault. It was before you were born. I grieve that the abuse was by our father. I know that your experience of our father was different than mine, and it is not my intent to take away your reality or your experiences. What I must do is be true to myself.

For too many years I kept "the secret". I did not do it very successfully in many ways, because I was deeply affected by what had happened in my childhood. Denying it caused me to act out in many ways, to hurt others and myself, to be less than I could be. My own therapeutic growth has been the single most important experience in my life — it has given me a chance to be me. But to ever be complete, I must be real, I must be honest. I want to say some things that are important. I am telling the truth when I tell you that I was abused as a child. I am not "crazy", that is, out of touch with reality, and no one is causing me to say and do the things I do — I am in charge of me.

Many persons have been a part of my recovery, I owe them much, but ultimately each of us must be responsible for our own choices. I take responsibility for mine. I have much more work to do on myself. I am far, far from being "all knowing" or even "all well." It is a lifelong process. But I do know that for me to con-

tinue to be healthy and live, I must no longer keep "the secret."
This does not mean that I need to talk about details and work out
things personally with anyone. I can and will do this in therapy.
But it does mean not pretending. It does mean being with people
who support me.

I want to be here for you, to help you understand me and the
way it was in our family. I will be here for you if you have ques-
tions or fears. I will be here for you for us to grow to know each
other. Our family has had a great deal of pain and fear. It also
has a great deal of love and potential for pulling together and being
real. It can be different for our children, we can break the cycle, we
can be an example. For me, that means being real, being honest,
being loving.

Thank you for listening (if you have read this far!) Much love
to you, little sister.

With love,
Claire

A VALUABLE LESSON

We wish that we could tell you that Claire's family read her letters and understood better what had happened to her and what she was doing to become healthy, and that they became a supportive part of her recovery program. Unfortunately, this did not happen. They perceived her letters as threatening and abusive and told her she was wrong to have written them.

Although Claire was saddened by her family's response, she was grateful that she had written down how she felt and that she had attempted to share it with them. In the process, she learned a valuable lesson. Convincing her family that she has been victimized, sharing childhood secrets, or even gaining their support and affirmation were not the most important goals of her letters. The most important goal and accomplishment was confronting the secrecy and shame she had lived with all her life.

She discovered that by speaking the truth and renouncing the shame and secrecy, she freed herself to be, for the first time in her life, free of shame.

Whatever modality you choose to deal with this part of your recovery program—by confronting your family and family friends in person, in writing, or in therapy—you can achieve the results that Claire did. You can learn how to let go of your childhood expectations of your parents and move on to a healing and healthy acceptance of yourself, your reality, and your family.

SOME FAMILY PERSPECTIVES:

A COUSIN:
I always thought there was something strange about him (the victimizer,) but I never knew what it was. I just never felt comfortable around him.

A BROTHER:
I remember that time you went to the hospital because you "fell off your bicycle" and got a concussion. It was when Mom was pregnant with brother.

A SISTER:
I always hated you because you got such special treatment. It seemed like Dad liked you best.

THE VICTIMIZER:
I never realized how much I hurt you. I was so ashamed, I thought that the best thing to do was to pretend that it never happened.

Be prepared for mixed reactions from family members and friends of the family if you decide to talk honestly about your abusive childhood. Some persons will be fearful, but will listen and be empathetic and supportive. Frequently, other family members were also abused but have never told anyone. Your honesty will present a time of stress and choice for them. If they choose to be courageous you will have the opportunity to experience affirmation and mutual support. Family members and friends may offer bits of information which come from their own lives and will relate to your own experiences. They may remember details from the past which will help you put together events as they really occurred. A more complete picture of the past will begin to form, and memories they were puzzling will now make sense. A brother or sister may remember events, behaviors or attitudes from the family which you have forgotten or repressed. Each person will have his or her own unique perception of family experiences, influenced by their own defense mechanisms, belief systems, and emotions.

Repressed memories can be triggered as you listen to new information and observe the behavior of persons as they are confronted with the family secrets. You will need to prepare yourself to deal with both your feelings related to the memories and your feelings related to the actual process of sharing the family secrets. To maximize understanding communication, approach relatives and friends in a structured, considerate fashion. Establish a plan for sharing that will have an optimum chance of succeeding. You may need to talk in structured settings for short periods of time and at widely spaced intervals. Recognize that you may need a neutral and reassuring environment with a qualified professional assisting to work through issues with those family members who are willing to face the truth. Your relationships with family members and friends will change in direct proportion to the degree to which each individual is supportive and courageous enough to face and work through the issues with you.

A YOUNGER SISTER:
The rest of you kids where all so much older than me. He always brought me special treats and told me that I was his little angel.

A YOUNGER BROTHER:
All I know is that I didn't like being at home. So I was gone a lot with sports and friends and stuff like that.

AN OLDER BROTHER:

I knew he had girlfriends, and that he treated Mom terribly, but I didn't want to admit it to myself. I heard people talk and I felt so ashamed, I just pretended it didn't exist, that it wasn't real.

THE VICTIMIZER:

I never knew how much it affected you. I thought you were O.K. because you never said anything was wrong.

Remember that each member of your family will have had his or her own unique experiences. Younger brothers or sisters may not have been abused or may not be aware of the ways in which they were abused or neglected. They may be in denial or delusion. Recognize that you all have the experience of a dysfunctional family in common, but the specific manifestations of that dysfunction will vary between family members. Each of you played a unique role in the family. Each of you has differing perceptions and experiences. Each of you has your own belief system. As the truth of the past unfolds, each family member will be confronted with her/his own issues. Courage and loving support can facilitate change, but each family member must work her own recovery program if she so chooses.

AN OLDER SISTER:

Why are you causing all this pain and difficulty? It happened to me too and I handled it O.K. without telling anyone. What happened was a long time ago. What good does it do to bring it up now?

A YOUNGER SISTER:

No, I don't know if I believe it's true or not! Why should I have to decide between you and Dad . . .? If it's true, why didn't you tell me a long time ago? What do you want from me anyway? Do you think you're the only one with problems?

A BROTHER:

How can you say these awful things about him when he's not even here to defend himself? Why didn't you say this when he was alive?

A MOTHER:

No, I don't remember those things happening. I don't think this therapy is doing you any good. I think you are getting worse! Why do you hate me after all the times I protected you from him?

A VICTIMIZER:

Can't you see that you are killing your mother by making these terrible accusations? How can you be so selfish and inconsiderate?

Behind the above reactions is the desire that you do not challenge the existence of denial and delusion that many family members have been living. They have utilized various coping mechanisms for a long time and you are now threatening their carefully constructed system of self-deception. Without denial, isolation, fantasy or other coping mechanisms, how will they face life They may fear going crazy, losing control, finding out that they are unlovable and imperfect and may now have to face great pain or sadness.

Realize that some family members may react with anger. They may become frightened and react by venting their fear on you. They may attack your capabilities as a reliable person, a mother, a sister, or a daughter. They may challenge your ability to distinguish fact from fiction and allude to any past aberrant behavior you may have exhibited as proof of your unreliability. They may question your motives. They may divert your attention from the abuse issues by placing you on the defensive. They may use arguments which are contradictory and confusing. They may ask questions and make accusations that are totally irrelevant to the real issues. They may imply that you are causing them and other family members unnecessary pain and suffering. They may accuse you of being the problem and shame you for willfully and selfishly disrupting their lives. Any or all of these behaviors are part of blaming the victim for the victimizer's behavior.

Some family members will use an approach/avoidance technique. On one day they will be supportive and caring. On another day they will be distant and indecisive. They may be persons who try to be all things to all people. They may never acknowledge the truth of the past. They may exhibit inconsistency in the presence of other family members, saying to each one what he or she most wants to hear. You will wonder about your own judgments and perceptions as you observe a person who appeared to believe you acting as if she does not when she talks with someone else. Your new-found sense of reality is being tested. Do not give it away. It is not you, but other persons who are avoiding reality.

A BROTHER:
Sure, I believe you that it happened, but why dwell on it? ("It" being multiple rape, broken bones and numerous concussions.) What are you bringing to the folk's house for dinner Sunday?

A MOTHER:
Honey, I don't think he meant to hurt you. You have to understand that he had such a problem with the booze and the pills. Why can't you just forget about all that unpleasantness and get on with your life?

A SISTER:
O.K., O.K., so it happened. So you went through hell. Now let go of it, will you? We all have problems!

A VICTIMIZER:
Look, I said I was sorry. What more do you want from me? I can't change the past. Haven't I always given you anything you asked for? I deserve some consideration, too.

Some family members may act as if nothing ever happened, that what you are saying is unimportant. They may verbally acknowledge what you say, but have little emotional reaction . . . no tears, anger, interest or concern. They will discourage your working things through and encourage you to minimize the importance of your experiences. They will tell you that they themselves have no problems from living in the family or that they are handling them in a discrete and appropriate way. They will explain to you that they have put the past behind them and are "just fine." And all the while they may be hiding or denying troubled marriages, alcoholism, workaholism, prescription drug use, stress-related illnesses or their inadequacies as parents.

You may choose to end some relationships. Some persons will choose to leave you. If you choose to maintain contact with persons from the past, you will need to give up the unrealistic image of them that you have held and the expectations of them which are part of those images. As long as you pursue affirmation or love from someone who is unwilling or unable to provide it, you are allowing yourself to be dependent upon that person. As long as you want or need someone else to tell you that you are worthwhile, sane or lovable, you are dependent on her/him and will limit your potential for growth and autonomy. In reality, some people will be supportive and some others will react with anger and fear.

Many persons will not want to know how you have been abused, and they will be even less interested in knowing how they might have played a part in your dysfunctional family system. They do not want to be reminded of their own experiences; they prefer the status quo. Incongruously, they may be people who cry at sad movies, agonize over tragedies in the newspapers and support worthwhile charities. They may describe themselves as sensitive, too sensitive, in their own minds, to have played a part in the suffering of others. When challenged to express caring to someone close to them, someone with whom they share some common issues and experiences, they will avoid the experience at any cost, and if necessary, attack to defend their carefully crafted version of reality. The reality of your abuse will be unacceptable and incomprehensible to them.

You will be surprised and gratified by some of the people who support you, and you will feel hurt and betrayed when some others abandon you. Often the family members whom you protected and admired the most will fail to support you (or actively sabotage your recovery), while persons you underestimated will exhibit courage and understanding you did not know they possessed. Gifts of support and love will appear from the most unlikely sources.

Practice constructive selfishness and protect yourself from further trauma and abuse. The process of confrontation and sharing childhood abuse needs to be carefully and responsibly conducted. This is your responsibility. Remember that your goal is to heal, not to hurt. Do it only when you are emotionally and psychologically ready to accept the consequences. You can responsibly take on such a formidable task only when you are willing to be honest and realistic with yourself and others. To ensure a successful and safe process, enlist the assistance of trusted friends and confidants and, if possible, professionals with expertise in dealing with childhood sexual abuse.

Throughout the process of informing and confronting relatives and friends, there are two important affirmations that you must practice on a daily, perhaps hourly, schedule:

(1) You are not responsible for the abuse that you experienced as a child. The person or persons who victimized you, who abused and misused you, are responsible.

(2) You are not responsible for the pain, fear, anger or any other discomfort that some people may experience as a result of your facing and sharing the truth of your abuse. It is the victimizer(s) who hid behind the secret and left you with the shame who must now be held accountable.

As the facade of the past crumbles and you practice speaking and living the truth, the family members and friends who believe in you will make themselves known. When you complete the process of letting go of your idealized images of your family of origin, you will be free to see them as the multidimensional individuals that they really are.

BECOMING WHOLE

On the journey of recovery you will experience a wide variety of emotions and psychological responses to the changes that are occurring in your life. Frequently these responses will seem dichotomous: joy and anger, trust and fear, pleasure and pain, attraction and aversion, reality and illusion, control and vulnerability, the presence of a higher power and the absence of a higher power. You will have many opportunities to practice testing and trusting your new-found sense of reality. These experiences are all parts of a wonderful phenomenon—that of becoming a whole person, of shedding the denial and delusion of the past and of embracing yourself as the unique and truly alive individual that you were born to be. In the process, you will uncover many deceptions and encounter many difficult truths.

It is a generally accepted maxim that all children love their parents and that they seek to have their needs met through the parent-child relationship: nurturance, approval, attention, a sense of "belonging" and significance in the family unit. Children are voracious human "sponges," soaking up verbal and non-verbal information and integrating what they learn into their perceptions of themselves and the world around them. It is the responsibility of parents to provide for their children the best lessons they can: teaching, sharing, modeling, facilitating, supporting and encouraging. Human beings are fallible. Every parent falls short of being a perfect parent; every parent will experience times when he or she will be unable to be an influence or make a difference.

You may experience feelings of fear, shame, pain and anger over the ways that your parents and other significant persons in your childhood, persons whom you loved and trusted, let you down and abused you. Recognizing their fallibility and reacting to it with pain, anger and/or sorrow does not mean that you have stopped loving them. It is not required that you stop loving them in order to be mentally healthy. If you face the truth—that they passed on to you both strengths and weaknesses— you will understand them more clearly. You may begin to free yourself to experience an even deeper appreciation and love for them. Loving them or not loving them, the choice is yours. It is a choice that you alone can make after considering what is best for you.

When we love distorted images of people, we do them an injustice. We do not allow them to be real, to be human. When we love a myth—an illusion we create to make life easier, less painful, or less frightening for ourselves or the other person—we miss knowing the real person. By denying reality, we miss the opportunity to learn how to maximize genuine sharing in our own lives and in the lives of our children. When we hold on to fantasy, denial and delusion, we not only deny others the opportunity to be real with us, but we also cannot allow our own imperfections to be known.

HEALTHY PARENTING

It is normal for a profound emotional and psychological bond to develop between parent and child, between father and daughter. The parenting role of a father, the enormous influence that he exerts over his child, is both a privilege and an awesome responsibility. To maximize healthy parenting, it is critical that a father or father-figure be knowledgeable about what is required of him as a parent, usually the most important role that he will play in the life of his child. He is a primary influence on her developing beliefs of self, relationships, and the world. He is a primary role-model for the men to whom she most likely will be attracted to in the future. It is his job to show her, through his behavior and attitudes toward her and other women, that he believes her to be a valued and respected human being, that she, as a whole person, is much more than her talents, faults, intellect, achievements, failures, abilities or sexuality. By loving her unconditionally, encouraging her, supporting her emotionally and physically, teaching her independence and confidence, he teaches her to trust herself to make choices which will enhance the quality of her life.

Whether he intends to or not, a father teaches his child, through his behaviors and attitudes, about sexuality and relationships. What she learns from him will contribute significantly to her own decisions about sexuality: whether to trust or distrust herself and others, to approach or avoid intimacy, to view sexuality as a shame-free dimension of every person or as a shameful secret to be hidden or avoided. If a father provides information and mature discussion in a shame-free approach and offers himself as a sensitive listener, she will learn many positive lessons. If he respects her personhood and does not abuse her trust, she is encouraged to trust and respect herself. If he teaches her, by example and affirmation, that her sexuality and the expression of it is but one dimension of her personhood, she will be empowered to appreciate herself and others as multidimensional, unique and valuable human beings.

The bond between mother and child is of equal profundity and power as the bond between father and child. Most of the lessons outlined above apply equally to the mother-daughter relationship. There are important similarities and differences. As a role-model, a mother teaches a child through her behaviors and attitudes what it means to be female. How a mother regards herself and others, both male and female, the attitudes and behaviors that she expresses and represses, her approval and disapproval— these factors and many others all influence the conclusions that a child makes about love, marriage, sex, relationships, etc. Honesty, compassion, vulnerability and a willingness to risk being known contribute to positive lessons for a child. Denial, dishonesty, hostility and shame contribute to other lessons. When parents take responsibility for both their successes and their failures as persons and as parents, they are preparing their children to do the same when they become adults. A wise old adage states that we need to give our children only two gifts: strong roots to be nurtured by and strong wings to fly away with.

FREEING YOURSELF FROM THE PAST

Identifying traumatic experiences in your childhood and understanding how they have influenced you is a vital step in freeing yourself from the tyranny of the past. When repressed or suppressed, the effects of past traumas influence your behavior and attitudes as an adult. They are acted out in addictive, compulsive behaviors, self-defeating attitudes, self-destructive and other-destructive behavior, continued victim mentality, and many other painful and self-defeating lifestyles. An aspect of life in which these negative effects most tragically surface is in the rearing of one's own children. The fear, pain, anger or shame that you as a parent avoid, condemns your own children to struggle with the trauma in their lives. The good news is that each fear and pain, each angry behavior or shameful attitude that you confront and work through in your own life ensures that the legacy you are passing on to your children will be free of repressed emotions.

Psychoanalyst Dr. Alice Miller, in her book *Thou Shalt Not Be Aware*, describes with clarity and power the reasons for, and value of, confronting the traumas of childhood rather than submerging them in denial and delusion:

Liberation and the ability to love are attained by experiencing traumatic childhood situations and articulating the resulting hatred and despair, not by acting them out. Only if these emotions are dissociated from their cause will they lead to destructive and self-destructive behavior. . .But if we succeed in working through our sorrow, we shall gain the freedom to judge for ourselves and with this the possibility and the right to make use of our own eyes and ears and to take our own perceptions seriously.

RE-PARENTING

Some persons will identify only a few areas in which members of their family of origin failed to prepare them adequately for adulthood. Some persons will be asked to accept the reality that they had little or no healthy, responsible parenting. Most of you will fit somewhere in between these two extremes. You may decide to seek out what we call a "parenting mentor" — a person who is willing and able to play the role of the healthy parent you never had. Share nourishing time together. Share activities that you both enjoy. This may be as simple as walks in the park or a cup of coffee at the kitchen table. Talk about yourself; risk discussing topics that you would not usually talk about. Share your "difficult" feelings — your sadness, your fears, your pain, your guilt, your shame. Ask for what you need, and listen and learn from someone you trust. Use your mentor-student relationship until you both decide that you are ready to "fly away on strong wings."

As you discard old habits and try on new ones, you will begin to notice that you are different, that you are changing. There will be tears, pain and sadness, but there will also be more moments of spontaneity, joy and peace. Tears of happiness as well as pain or sorrow will burst forth, and your own laughter will surprise you with its naturalness and genuineness. These are all indicators that the child within you is being reborn. You are becoming healthy and whole. Love and cherish your perfect and innocent child. Affirm and celebrate that you are choosing life, not death. We believe that it is never too late to have a happy childhood.

SELF-DISCOVERY

You will encounter many milestone experiences on the road of recovery. Some examples are: when you acknowledge the abuse as a shame-free reality, when you face the issues in your life that keep you from being well, such as addiction and co-dependency, and when you seek professional help on your recovery journey.

Personal milestones will be unique and relative to each individual traveler. Within the growth process of every individual, however, milestones will occur. It is important that you recognize and celebrate them. Milestones are intended to stay with us. They may occur for only moments at a time or they may be sustained for long periods of time and become part of a new life-style. Milestones occur as a person moves from the path of "resolution of past traumas" to the path of "self-discovery."

The resolution path is typified by (1) understanding the role the past has played in bringing the person to this point in her life and (2) doing the necessary "work" to let go of the past and commit oneself to the present and the future. It is a path which shows an individual her weaknesses and her errors. It shows her the faulty thinking, the habituated patterns of behavior, and the shame with which she has been handicapped.

DISCOVERING YOUR HIDDEN CHILD WITHIN

As the learned behaviors and attitudes of the past are understood and the unresolved emotional issues surrounding them are confronted and resolved, the traveler moves into a new dimension: that of discovering the child within her who has been hidden from her awareness all these years. She begins to try new experiences; she learns to identify and trust her own sense of reality. The internal messages of the past no longer exert a controlling influence over her. She becomes increasingly more free to choose her path in life. She no longer needs to compulsively please others. She practices pleasing herself. She evaluates information and experiences and decides what philosophy, what school of thought, and what structure of spirituality fits for her. She is no longer a victim.

A milestone that may at first last only for brief periods of time can, with practice, grow into a sustained state of being. As she grows in strength and rids herself of the influences of the past, she experiences with increasing frequency and prolonged duration the joy of being the person she was born to be. It is a new and sometimes frightening phenomenon. Because it is unfamiliar, she sometimes mistakenly identifies it as something negative. She may run from it or sabotage herself. If she is committed to growth, however, she will be gentle and patient with herself; she will persist on her journey. She will courageously and determinedly involve herself in activities and relationships which facilitate her "being herself."

Deciding which behaviors and attitudes are a result of the abuse of the past and which are a result of "normal" learning experiences is not a simple or clear-cut process. It requires diligent self-examination and trusting others to give you honest feedback about what they see in various situations. Each of us must accept that, if we choose health, we will spend our lifetime in the process of attaining and maintaining it. There is not a clear-cut, identifiable line to be crossed when one resolves the past, nor is there a smooth path of uninterrupted self-discovery. Often it is two steps forward and one step backward.

FREEDOM

If you determinedly and consistently work a strategy for personal growth, if you, as we say, "work a program," there will come a time when the abuse will be an acknowledged part of your history but it will no longer control you — it will not dominate your total identity. Perceiving oneself as no longer a victim is a powerful and nourishing experience; take time to celebrate each time you recognize it. It is true that your abuse was real and influenced your life for many years. It is true that because of it you missed out on many important aspects of life to which every child has a birthright. At times, you will still experience sadness and anger about how you were tricked and cheated. It was not fair that you were abused. It is human to wish that it had been different. Part of your recovery program is to mourn your losses and move on. One of the goals of recovery is that the abuse no longer dominates your attitudes and behaviors; that it no longer exerts a controlling influence over you.

Growing beyond the abuse you suffered as a child is part of the process of maturation. You will at times confront the reality that in many ways you are reaching a higher level of maturity than many of the people around you. You may be frightened or saddened by this realization, at times you may even yearn to go back to the way it used to be.

It is difficult to leave old friends behind. Wisdom and maturity are responsibilities that often feel heavy and difficult. Attaining some measure of them means that we can no longer use the excuse of ignorance or lack of ability to avoid responsibility for our own lives. It is regrettable that many persons never have the courage to look at the realities of their lives, let alone embark on the perilous journey of growth and self-discovery. Too many persons are born, live and die behind a veil of denial, delusion and ignorance. They decide to believe that they have "no problems" and therefore have no need for self-examination or change. Be aware that if you decide to embark on a journey of self-discovery and change, you will have chosen, to borrow the title of M. Scott Peck's book, *The Road Less Traveled.*

I AM

If the members of a group of "average" women were each asked to "Describe yourself in one sentence.", the responses might be as follows: "I am a wife and mother,"; "I am a teacher,"; "I am a sensitive and loving person,"; "I am tall and blond like my Swedish parents." In follow-up statements each woman might go on to explain that there are many other dimensions she could use to describe herself. The first statement of self that a person makes, however, is probably the most revealing and most powerful. When we identify with a group, a role or a descriptor, we automatically restrict ourselves from knowing and accepting other parts of ourselves.

It is critical that you recognize and affirm that you are much more than any role(s) you play in life. You are much more than any life event in which you participated. You are much more than any disturbing emotions or thoughts you have experienced, much more than your physical attribute, much more than your behaviors or attitudes. The moment you state, "I am a victim," you have defined yourself in constricting terms. Perhaps you were a victim; perhaps you experienced abuse as a child; perhaps you still are influenced or controlled by those early life experiences. You are, however, much more than those experiences.

A valuable part of any recovery program involves daily affirmations. Affirmation involves stating something positively, accepting your statements as valid and dedicating yourself to upholding and practicing them. There is personal power in communicating with positive messages. Affirmations must be practiced on a regular basis to be effective. There are times when the influences of one's external world seem stronger than one's internal reality. Persons who have been abused have been taught to give away their own reality, not to trust themselves or their perceptions. Find a time each day to practice affirming yourself. Make this time a priority. You are worth it. In your own private, special time, give yourself messages of love and support.

AFFIRMATIONS FOR GROWTH AND LOVE

You may choose to use some of the following affirmations in your recovery program, or there may be others that you find nourishing and helpful. Choose affirmations that you are able to believe in, affirmations that you want to believe in, affirmations that facilitate your growth and recovery program. During the time you choose to practice your affirmations, close your eyes and imagine yourself surrounded in safety and love.

I AM the center of my life; all else revolves around me.

I AM lovable; only if I love myself first will I be able to love others.

I AM capable of expressing love and allowing myself to be loved.

I AM a channel for love; the empathy I give to others, I also give to myself.

I AM willing to be vulnerable to others that I love and trust, but I will not allow anyone to abuse me.

I AM willing to be honest, but I will not use my honesty to deliberately hurt another person.

I AM a person of many dimensions—emotions, thoughts, body and spirit.

I AM in touch with my feelings; I will not deny any feeling, as they are all of equal value.

I AM in touch with my body, I will treat it with respect and appreciation.

I AM a spiritual being; I will surrender to my higher power.

I AM a sexual being; I rejoice in my sexuality and respect my femaleness.

I AM connected to all other life; we are each parts of a whole.

I AM in control of my recovery; it is from responsible behavior and attitudes that growth occurs.

I AM responsible for my recovery and growth; I accept this responsibility.

I AM participating in a lifelong process of growth; I will open myself to the lessons that are all around me.

I AM a being of great potential and promise; the more I risk, the more I grow.

I AM a being of self-power and self-control; my life is enriched by this knowledge.

I AM joyful in each step of growth; the discovery of myself overwhelms me with happiness.

Do something each day to treat yourself well, to affirm your love of yourself. It may be as simple as listening to a bird singing in the park, a hot bath, allowing some time to begin a new book. It may be as profound as enrolling in a college class or deciding to face a new issue in your recovery program.

VICTORY

Throughout this text, the term "victim" has been used many times. By this point, the reader may be saturated with the terminology of sexual abuse. It is unfortunate that it is necessary in this educational process to communicate repetitiously so many painful or negative phrases. We hope that we have achieved a goal of also using positive words and phrases. We wish to describe not only the problems but also the solutions. Do not let the prevalence of the term "victim" mislead you. You were a victim; you are now in recovery. You were powerless; you are now empowered. Life was out of your control; you are learning how to take that power back. The fact that you are reading this book means that your recovery has begun. With each step you take, you become more an actor than a reactor. With each success you experience, you become more real and confident. You are no longer powerless, out of control, or defective.

YOU ARE NO LONGER A VICTIM, YOU ARE VICTORIOUS.

CONCLUSION

Commit yourself to living with a courage you are not sure you have.
THE AUTHORS

In writing this book we hope to accomplish two major objectives. One is remedial: To provide information and direction that will assist victims, and their families and friends to overcome the effects of childhood sexual abuse. The second is preventative: To stimulate awareness, research, and action which will decrease and eventually eliminate the trauma which is the result of childhood sexual abuse. Child abuse is a problem that affects not only the primary victim, the child, but the entire family, often for two or more generations. The phenomenon of child abuse is a problem which impacts our entire societal family as well. We must remedy the dysfunctions both within the individual abusive family system and on a broader, societal level. To facilitate healing and growth requires honesty and courage, as individuals and as a society.

You may remember that in the preface of this book we presented twelve questions that are frequently asked about childhood sexual abuse. Throughout the text we have endeavored to respond to them.

Here is a review of the questions and our answers:

QUESTION ONE:
Is sexual abuse a problem of major proportions in this country?

ANSWER:
Yes. As many as 32 million American women have had sexually abusive childhood experiences with an adult.

QUESTION TWO:
Is a person who was sexually abused as a child by an adult always influenced by that experience?

ANSWER:
Yes. Children use life experiences to form internalized belief systems about self, relationships, and the world. Sexual abuse influences the belief of one's sexual self and one's role in intimate relationships.

QUESTION THREE:
Is it possible for a person to be a victim of abuse and not remember the abuse or not identify it as abusive?

ANSWER:
Yes. Repressed memories of childhood abuse are common. Much abusive behavior is camouflaged as discipline, instruction, or affection.

QUESTION FOUR:
Can a single sexual abuse experience as a child cause problems for an individual as an adult?

ANSWER:
Yes. Any incident causing strong emotional reactions of fear, pain, shame, anger, or guilt can influence a person for years after the event.

QUESTION FIVE:
Can a person be sexually abused without being touched?

ANSWER:
Yes. A person's concept of her sexuality can be profoundly influenced by non-verbal and verbal communications, shaming messages, neglect and abandonment.

QUESTION SIX:
Can a person appear to be successful outwardly—be involved in a primary monogamous relationship; have close friends, children and

family; be sexually active; successfully pursue a career — and also be suffering with problems caused by an abusive childhood?

ANSWER:

Yes. A victim of abuse can sublimate her energies in work or family. She can repress or suppress the memories of her abuse. She can perform physically sexually but still be handicapped by the effects of the abuse.

QUESTION SEVEN:

Can sexual abuse as a child affect a person's adult sexuality and sexual lifestyle?

ANSWER:

Yes. It can cause an aversive reaction to the experience of specific sexual acts or to sexual behaviors and attitudes in general.

QUESTION EIGHT:

Can sexual abuse as a child affect areas of a person's adult life other than sexuality?

ANSWER:

Yes. It can influence the lessons that she teaches to her own children, what she thinks of herself as a person, and the manner in which she relates to one partner or to men in general.

QUESTION NINE:

Are there ways to tell the difference between healthy and unhealthy sexual contact between a child and an adult?

ANSWER:

Yes. Healthy adult sexual contact with a child is age-appropriate. The adult respects the child and does not exploit or abuse her by treating her as an adult.

QUESTION TEN:
Is there such a thing as "victim mentality"?

ANSWER:
Yes. A person victimized as a child learns how to be a victim and how to victimize. She will develop a belief system that reinforces victim attitudes and behaviors.

QUESTION ELEVEN:
Can an individual's sense of personal spirituality or her concept of God be affected by childhood sexual abuse?

ANSWER:
Yes. A child's concept of God is usually that of a male authority of unlimited power and knowledge. A child abused by a male authority figure may have difficulty developing a healthy spiritual life for herself.

QUESTION TWELVE:
Can a person triumph over the problems caused by an abusive childhood?

ANSWER:
Yes. The women in this book are a testimony to that truth. There are countless others working their own problems of recovery around the country, rising from the ashes of abuse to the joy of healing and wholeness.

       If you have read to this point, you have traveled a demanding road. The facts surrounding childhood sexual abuse are tragic and painful to confront. The life stories in the text are not abstract conjecture or theories. They are about real people and real situations. Many are stories that began in tragedy and ended in triumph. All of the women in the book were victims who sought answers and remedies for the problems that made them less effective, unhappy persons. As the reality of childhood sexual abuse reaches a higher level of awareness in the public's eye, as the shame of abuse is placed with the victimizer rather than the victim, more and more persons will find the courage to step forward and acknowledge their victimization. Men and women already on the road to recovery will serve as role models for others just beginning their journeys. Childhood sexual abuse knows no ethnic, socio-economic or religious boundaries; it occurs at all levels, within all cultures. It is encouraging to see, in recent years, that people of celebrity status and persons in authoritative leadership positions are risking the ramifications of public opinion and beginning to "go public" with the secret of their abuse.

Secrets control. As long as sexual abuse cannot be talked about, acknowledged or confronted, it will hold power over victims and victimizers alike. As long as we deny the pain, the suffering, and the wasted lives that result from being victimized, we will be severely limited in our growth as individuals and as a society. Fear, ignorance, shame and apathy are stones in the walls which block progress. Denial, delusions and deception are the mortar. Stone by stone, by individual effort and by group endeavor, the walls must be torn down.

YOUR BLUEPRINT FOR RECOVERY

Each person must design her own individualized recovery plan. Each timetable is as unique and individual as the person who follows it. Not everyone who was abused as a child will require professional intervention. Some or all of the following steps will be necessary ingredients in a successful recovery program. With the help of trusted and competent persons, decide which ones fit for you.

(1) Develop a support system. Supportive persons may be found in the community, such as in churches or synagogues, schools and social service agencies. Affirmation can also come from family members and friends. Have the courage to reach out and share your secret with a trusted other.

(2) Decide whether you need professional assistance, and seek out the most competent person you can find. If one therapist doesn't feel right to you, try another. Check out your impressions with someone you believe to be trustworthy. Ask for what you need.

(3) Identify your belief system: the beliefs that you learned in your family of origin. Recognize how it has affected your adult attitudes and behaviors.

(4) Until we confront the pain of the past, we are doomed to relive it again and again. Confront unresolved childhood issues and lay them to rest.

(5) Identify your habituated defense mechanisms and how you use them to avoid intimacy and pain. Practice new behaviors instead.

(6) Identify your cue responses — the momentary experiences which trigger emotional reactions — that are connected to your abuse. Learn and practice strategies for minimizing or eliminating their power over you in the present.

(7) Affirm your worth as a person. Remember that you are not defined by your abuse; your intrinsic value is much, much greater than anything that has been done to you.

(8) Learn and practice behaviors and attitudes that maintain a positive self-image.

(9) Identify any compulsive behaviors that require treatment — addictions, co-dependency — and enroll in appropriate recovery programs for them.

(10) Be gentle, patient and loving with yourself. It has taken you a lifetime to learn to live as you have in the past. Give yourself the rest of your life to learn a new and healthier lifestyle.

One of the results that comes from working a recovery program is freedom — freedom from shame, freedom from the control of others, freedom from habitual self-defeating behaviors and attitudes, and freedom from the debilitating lessons that were taught to you in the past. One of the gifts of recovery is the realization that you have the freedom to choose to be vulnerable, to love oneself, to successfully express emotions, and to mature in one's spirituality. Recovery and self-discovery are a lifetime process. None of us achieves perfection, but each of us deserves the opportunity to be better — healthier, happier, more functional persons. Life is a series of decisions. There may have been a time in our lives when we did not believe that we had any choices, when other persons controlled us. Through the process of recovery and self-discovery we can achieve the maturity to take control of our own lives and accept the responsibility for the decisions that we make. It is our hope that this book will assist you on your journey to freedom and maturity.

Comments regarding WITHOUT CONSENT, inquiries about Jeff and Carol's workshops, and requests to be on their mailing list may be sent to:

Jarvis & Kirkendall
P.O. Box 2956
Chino Valley, AZ 86323
Ph: (520) 636-8854
E-mail: dreamr@futureone.com